MIRROR

ELAINE WILSON

for Sheila Colquhoun & John Wilson

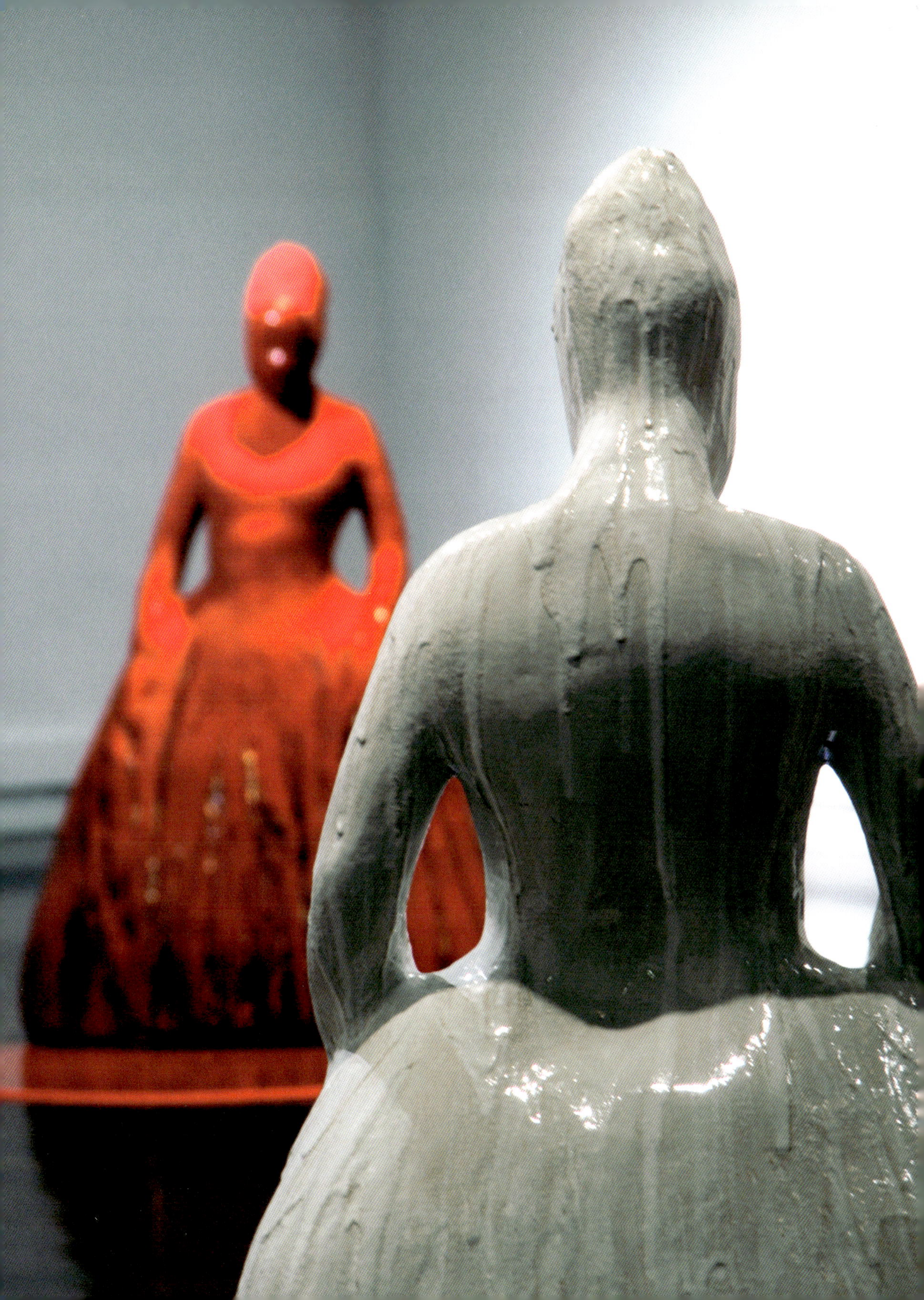

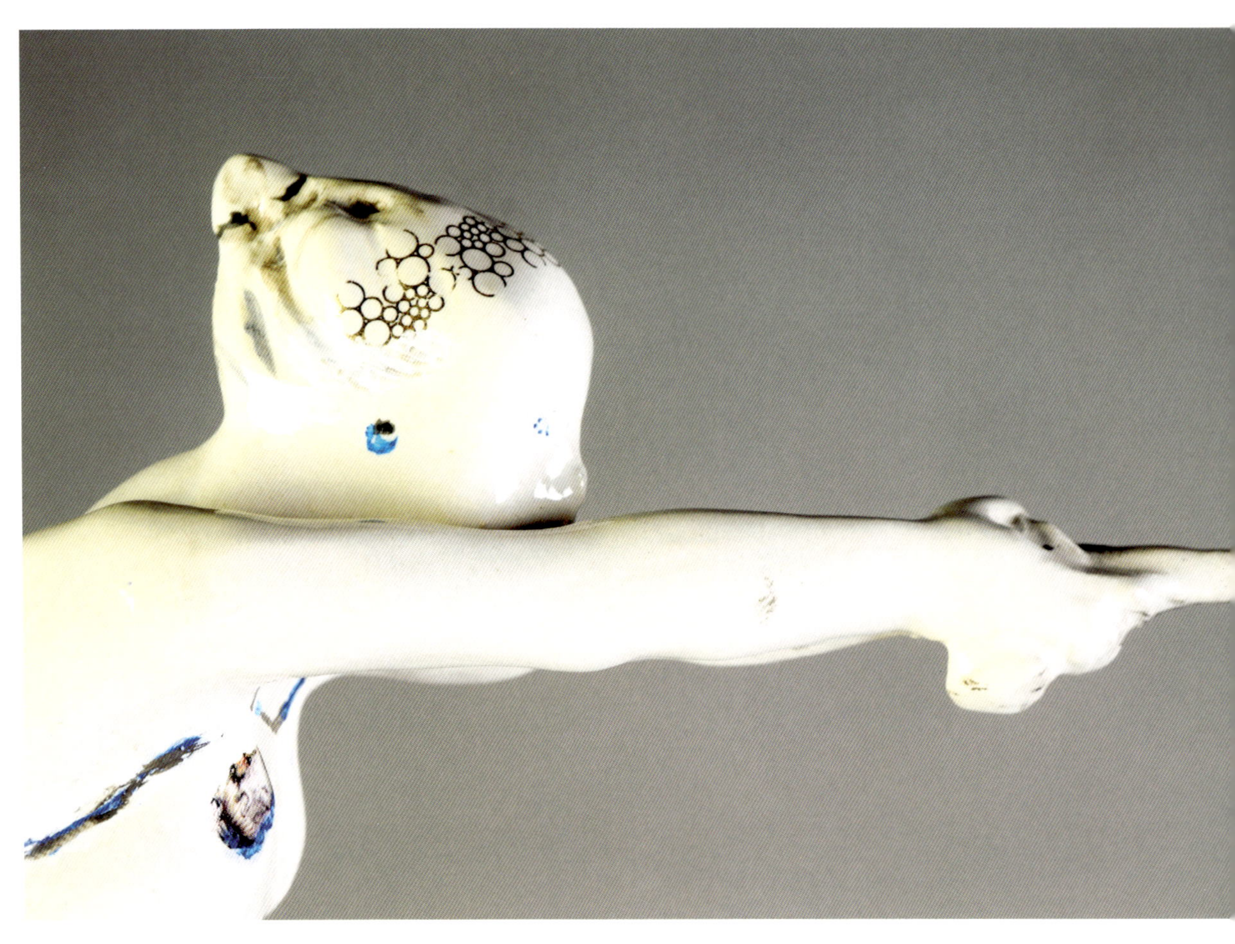

Previous: *Seeing Myself Seeing*, 2009, fired clay, decals, perspex

 Above: *Don't Touch !* 2009, (detail) fired clay, glaze, lustre, decals

FOREWORD

This publication places Elaine Wilson's work within both a contemporary and historic canon of fine art. As the contributors to this monograph so clearly illustrate, this work reaches deep into the history and traditions of art and literature and in so doing resonates an intangible familiarity. The forms suggest paintings once seen, the images, objects faintly remembered. Yet the works presented achieve something quite rare in contemporary art practice; they draw closely together art, artist and viewer.

Whether it's the liquid surface fired into a solid sheen or the layered collages sealed beneath resin, the work always communicates its surface and materiality. Describing Elaine Wilson's work in terms of its surface and process is to acknowledge its role in coercing and seducing the viewer into a gradual awareness of its subtle politics. This uneasy tension between the artworks and their references to ornament transgresses the public space of the art gallery to the private space of the domestic mantelpiece placing contested notions of gender, femininity and ornament at the heart of the work.

To work within the terms of the Renaissance sculptor or the eighteenth-century Royal Academician painter is a fearless thing to do. To bring to those terms such quiet commentary on femininity, domesticity, and the condition of being a contemporary female artist is inspired.

Trevor Keeble BA. MA.PHD (RCA) Associate Dean, Kingston University.

Keeble studied for an MA in the History of Design at the Royal College of Art and the Victoria and Albert Museum. He has completed a PhD (RCA) entitled, The Domestic Moment: Design, Taste and Identity in the Late Victorian Interior.

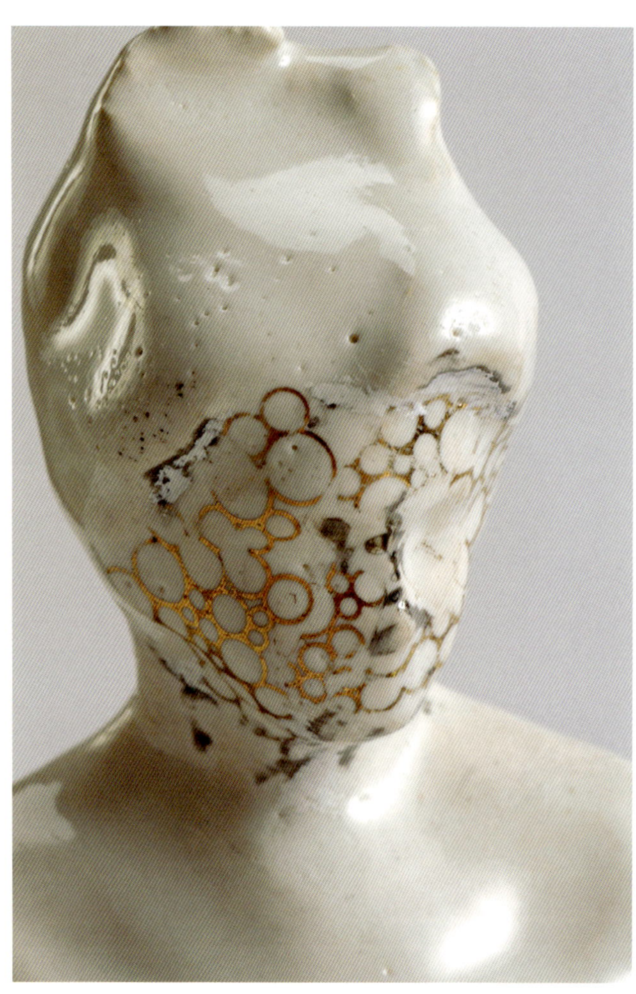

Opposite & above: *No Use Crying over Spilled Milk*, 2009, fired clay, glaze, decals, metal table, hand mirror

 Over: *Don't Touch !* 2009, fired clay, glaze, lustre, decals

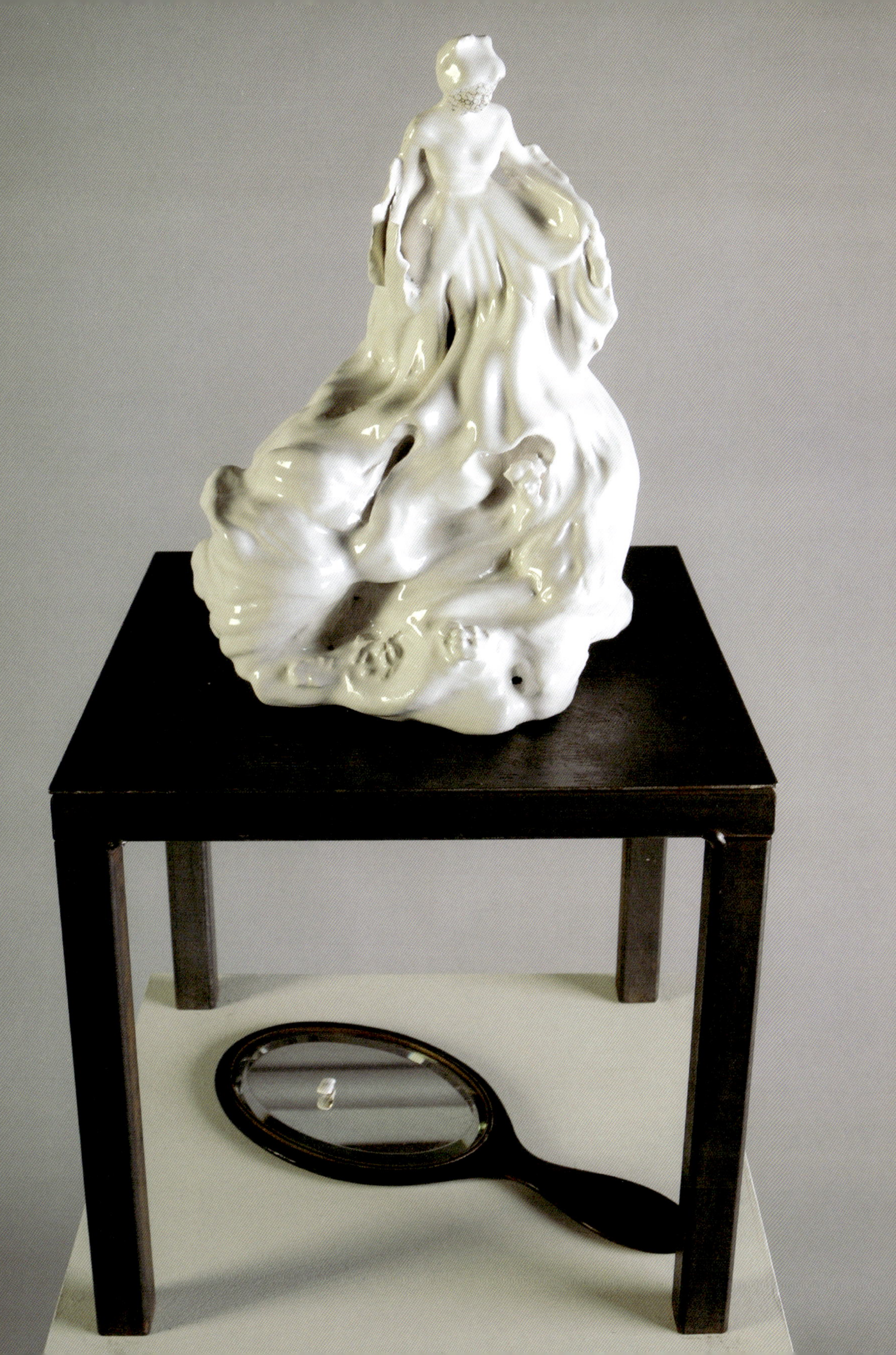

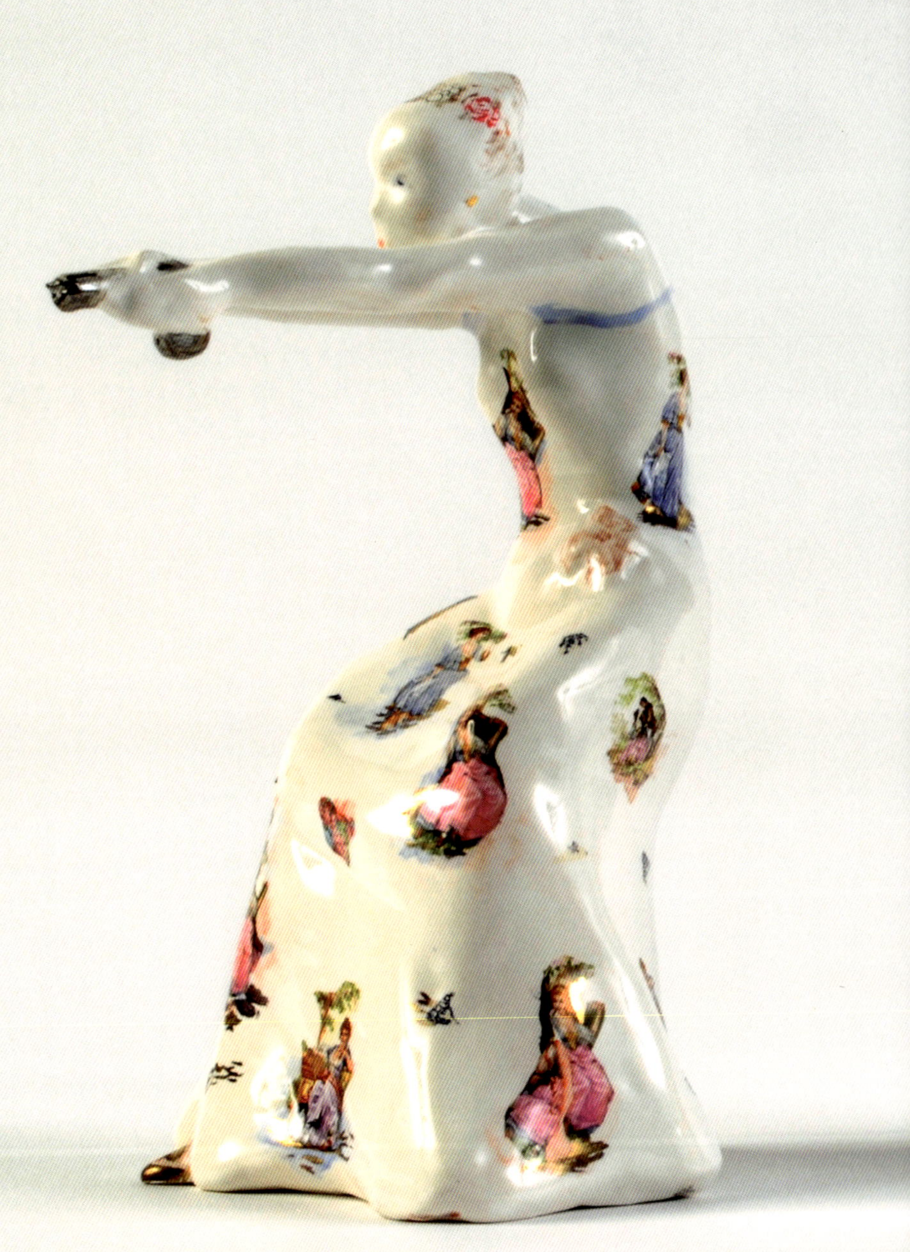

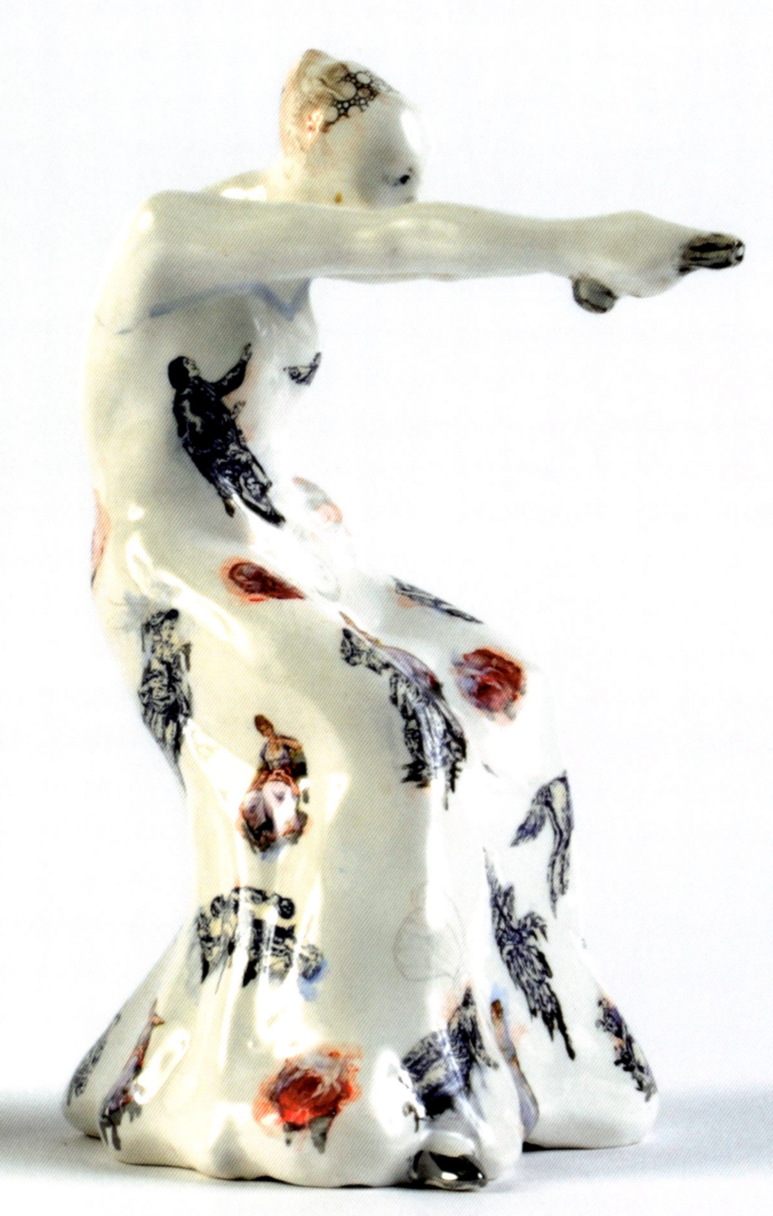

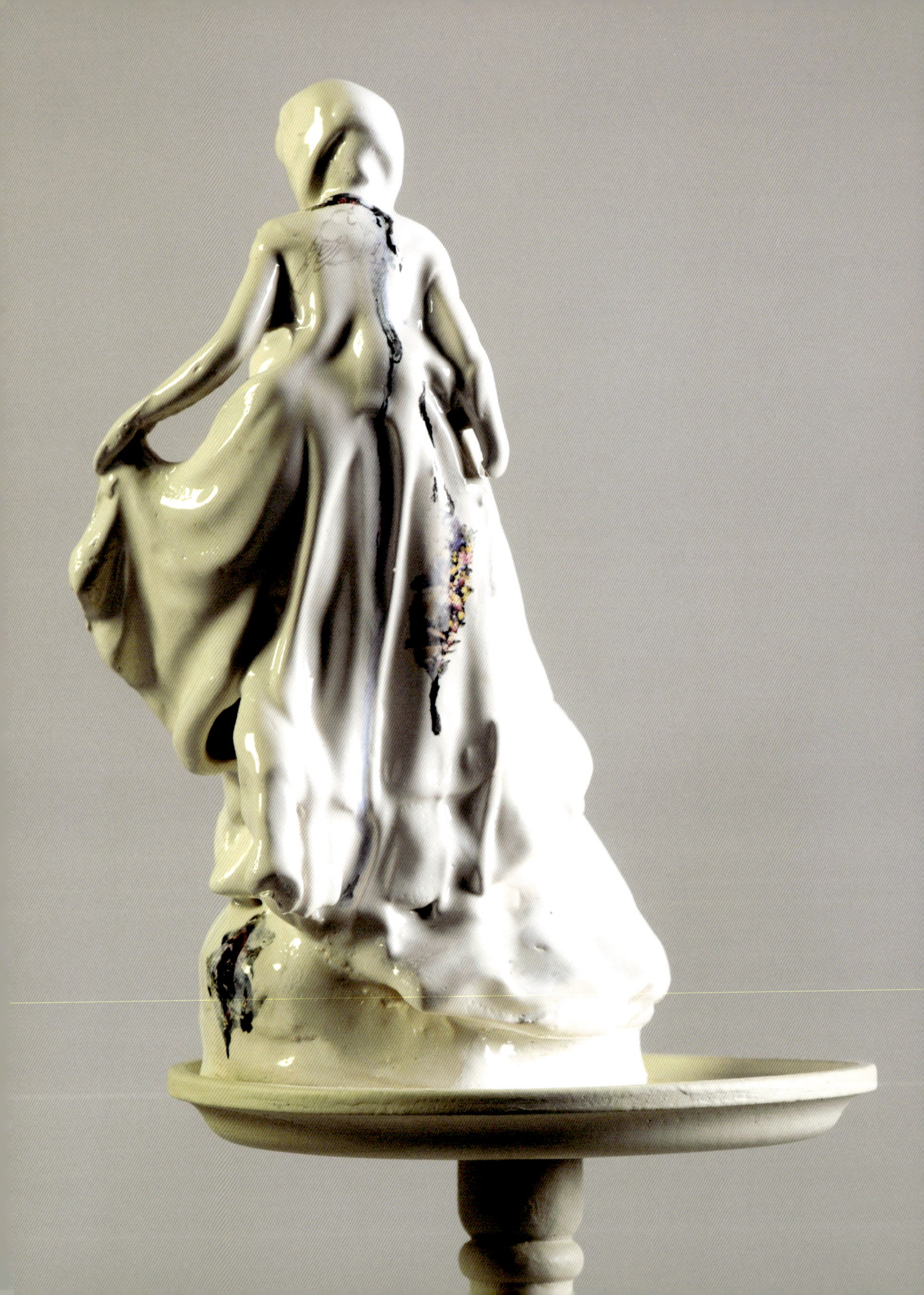

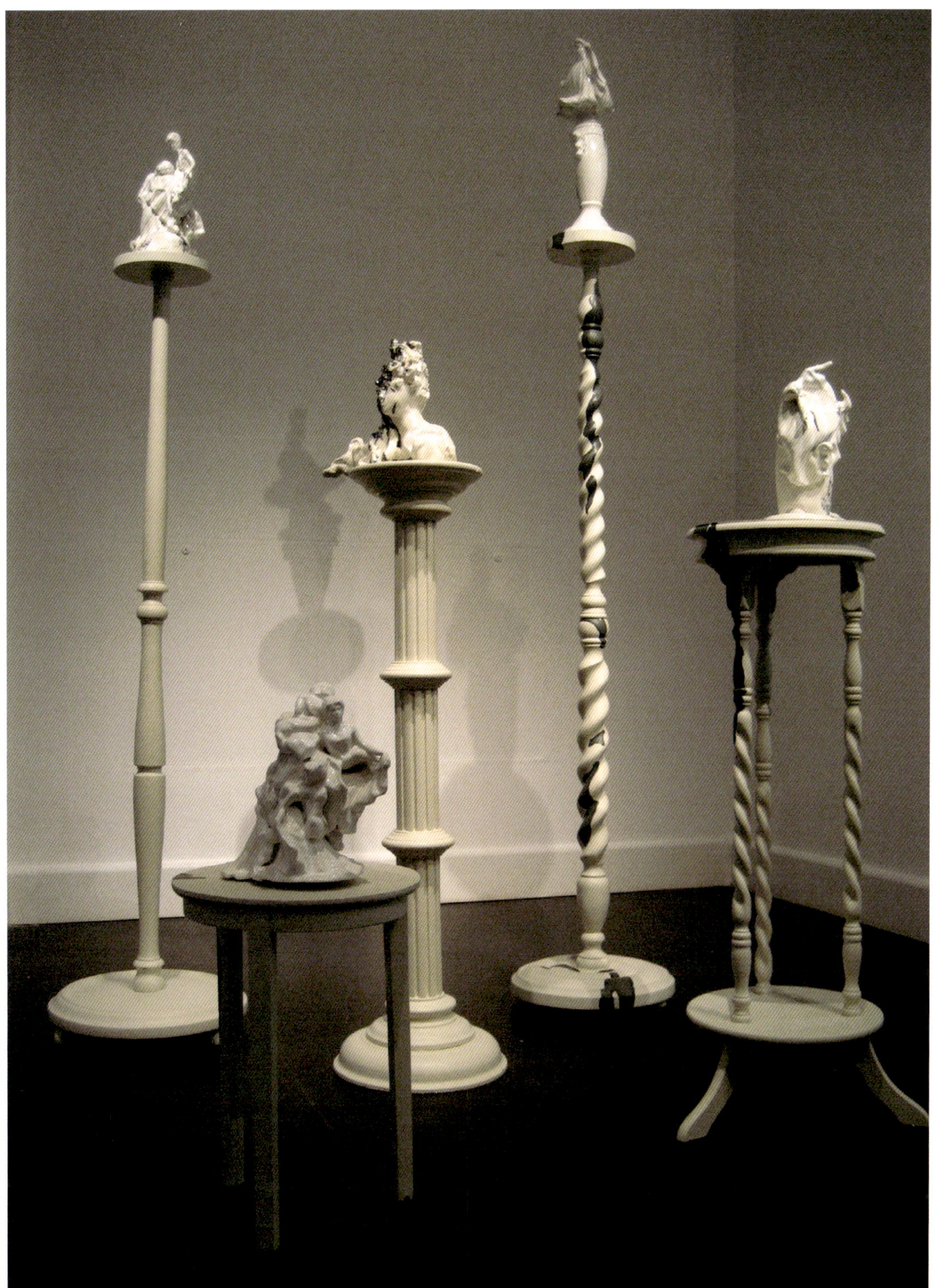

 Previous & opposite: *Fleurs du Mal Series*, 2008-9, fired clay, glaze decals, lustre, wooden plant stands

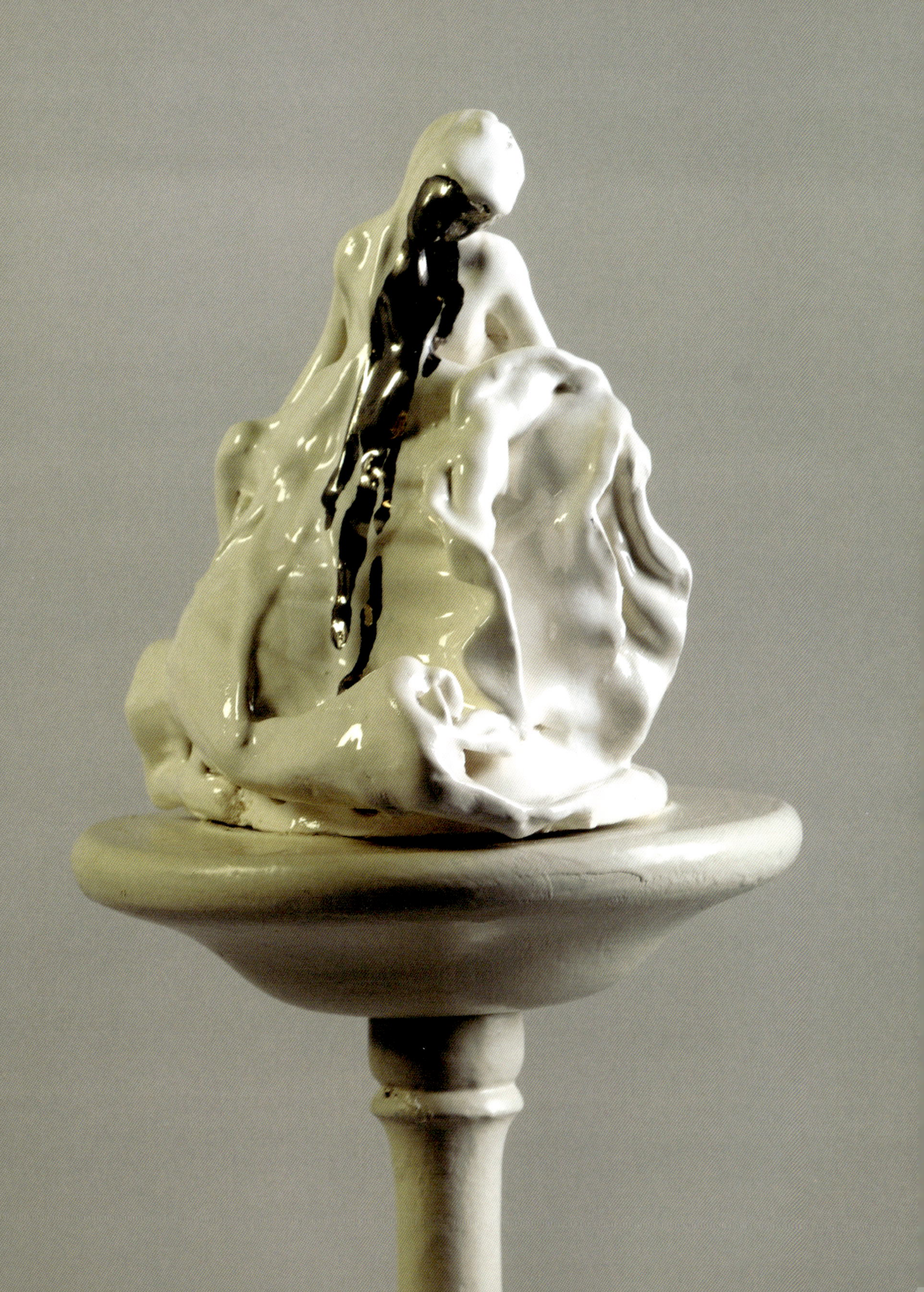

14 Opposite & over: *Fleurs du Mal Series*, 2008-9, fired clay, glaze decals, lustre, wooden plant stands

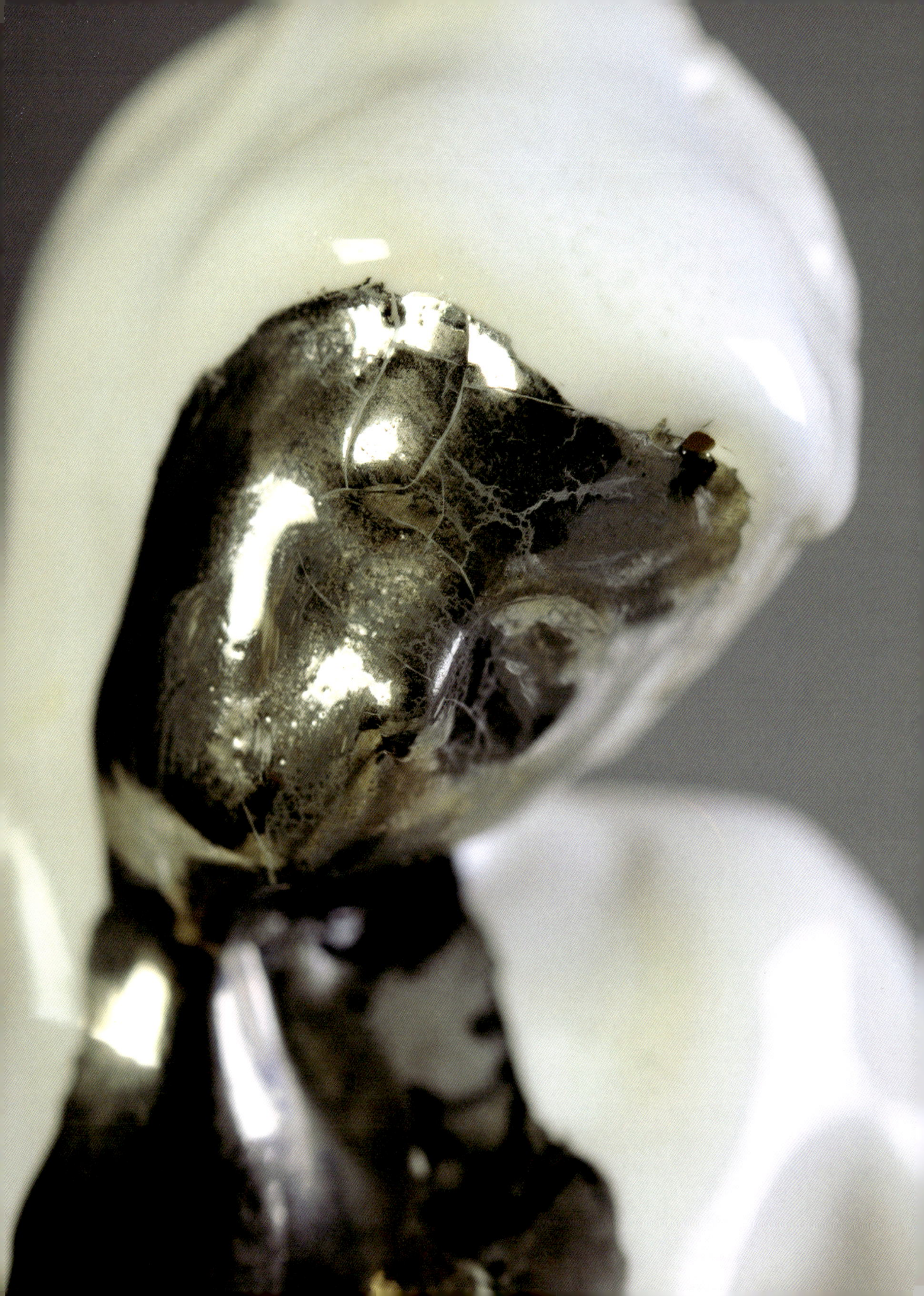

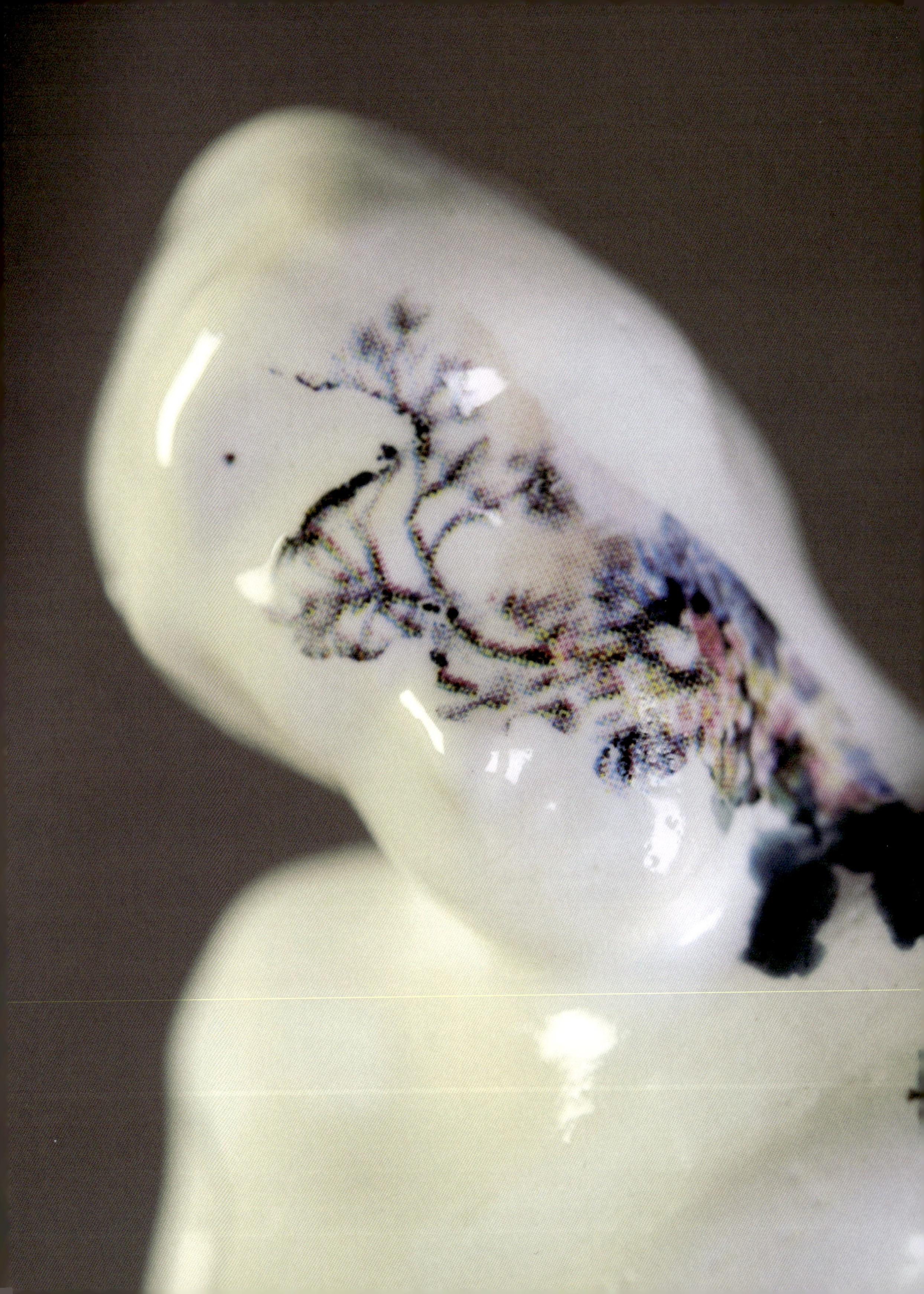

MIRROR, MIRROR

Mirror, mirror on the wall
Who is the fairest of them all?

In his seminal book *Ways of Seeing* John Berger famously claimed: "A man's presence suggests what he is capable of doing to you or for you. His presence may be fabricated, in the sense that he pretends to be capable of what he is not. But the pretence is always towards a power which he exercises on others.....By contrast, a woman's presence expresses her own attitude to herself, and defines what can and cannot be done to her.....One might simplify this by saying: *men act and women appear.* Men look at women. Women watch themselves being looked at.....Thus she turns herself into an object...."

Turning ourselves into objects is what women have been good at for centuries. Defined by the male gaze we have become locked into a solipsistic relationship with our physical selves. The mirror tells us who we are, that we exist, how the world sees us and, as a result, how we see ourselves. It is our confidante, our confessor, our friend and our critic, watching over our youthful blooming through to the daily process of slow decay. It is the barometer by which we gage every shift and nuance of our physical selves. Narcissus could never have been a woman with a gaze so replete with self-love. A woman's gaze, by contrast, is full of anxiety. Am I pretty enough, thin or young enough? "Mirror, mirror on the wall, who is the fairest of them all?" intoned Snow White's 'wicked' stepmother anxiously, knowing that her fading pre-menopausal looks were about to be usurped by her step-daughter's burgeoning beauty.

In Tennyson's poem *The Lady of Shallot*, the lady in the tower knows that a curse will befall her if she looks down to Camelot. Thus, she concentrates solely on her weaving, never lifting her eyes. However, as she weaves, a mirror hangs before her. In this, she is able to see "shadows of the world." Feminist critics have argued that the poem is concerned with women's sexuality and their place in the Victorian world. Moreover the Lady of Shalott's view of reality depends on the reflection she perceives in her mirror. Mirrors duplicate the scene they reflect, but images in mirrors are different to reality. They reverse the subject and relegate it to two dimensions. The objects reflected in the mirror cannot hurt the Lady of Shalott with the power of objects viewed directly. The reflected scenes of the Camelot countryside are further altered by her artistic imagination, as she incorporates them into her tapestry – a traditional form of female craft and expression. Thus the Lady is also presented as an artist, more involved in her creative version of her indirect experience than with life itself. Reality, as she knows it, is flat but gives the sense of depth. By transforming that reality, imaginatively, with her bright threads, she turns it into art. Yet when faced with actual reality by looking out the window, she breaks the mirror which she no longer needs and destroys her handiwork. Reality makes the art she has created vanish. Thus for a female artist the mirror becomes not just a facet of her own sexual and social view of herself but also a symbol of her desire to fill the blank surface of herself with artistic interpretations, a site of tension between the demands of the 'actual' world with its social and domestic demands, and the world of the imagination.

Using the language and tradition of ornamental sculpture and figurines the artist Elaine Wilson explores received notions of women and femininity, as well as the perpetuation of romantic and stereotypical ideals. In her *Seeing myself Seeing 2009*, two, not quite life sized, ceramic figurines that borrow something from Velázquez's Las Meninas, gaze into reflected pools of gloss colour. Their eyes are lowered, their gaze transfixed on the reflective surfaces beneath them. What selves are they seeing in the mirrored other? Splitting, doubling and magical thinking are all part of the female psyche, despite the dogmas of feminism that have done nothing to change the deep psychological ambivalence most women feel about themselves and their bodies. The public self and the secret self, the good girl and the bad, the Madonna and whore are all tropes that resonate within these two contrasting figures of virginal white and flagrant red porcelain. Separated by neurotic anxiety neither can embrace nor encompass the other self to become an organic whole. Each is doomed to be defined by the image reflected back to her from the mirror.

The theme of self and the 'other' is continued in Elaine Wilson's series of small slip-cast female figurines that precariously balance on plant stands like kitsch objects in a bourgeois sitting room. Taking as their title Baudelaire's decadent symbolist poem, *Fleurs du Mal*, these little figures, tattooed and decorated with cut and reassembled ceramic transfers of romantic pastoral scenes, appear to be melting to the point of collapse. Issues of memory and nostalgia, of decorum, pastiche and masquerade flirt, here, with notions of manufactured and mass produced images of woman. There is, about these small figures, a touch of Venice Carnival decadence, for they seem dressed to bemuse and confuse. In *No Use Crying Over Spilled Milk 2008*, a young girl fashioned in white porcelain, reminiscent of a capo di monte figurine, appears to be transmuting into the flowing folds of her voluminous dress, her identity utterly subsumed and defined by her attire. It is as if her body is dissolving, her messy corporeal self - one that menstruates and defecates - sanitised by her transmogrification from body into gown. She has no features; her face has become a mere web of anodyne silver glaze.

In antithesis, the witty little figure *Don't Touch! 2008*, offers an image of a young woman in a low cut ball dress - decorated with Joshua Reynolds style transfers of shepherdesses and bonneted ladies - crouched and ready to fire a pointed pistol. Like some poor little rich girl she erupts at being judged by the very signs that have come to define her. She is the

Patty Hearst of the porcelain world, the Sarah Palin of figurines. In a playful pun on Freudian penis envy, her fetishisation of the tool of male desire is turned back on the male viewer and his defining gaze.

Such 'feminist' views are, of course, no longer fashionable. For younger women feminism is seen as a puritanical restriction; one that debars sexy clothes, make-up or shaved legs; while flaunting one's cleavage is seen as 'empowering'. Of course, both this revisionist post-feminism, along with earlier fundamentalist precepts are equally misguided. For how women view themselves, and how they are viewed by others, is still a dominant social construct resulting in bulimia, anorexia, extreme dieting and excessive plastic surgery. It is this territory that Elaine Wilson makes her own. With wit and intellectual rigour she revisits the abiding female occupation with self-imagine, self-reflection, self-awareness and self-definition. In this she is much indebted to the works of Joan Riviera, who worked for Freud, and to the Israeli analyst, writer and artist Bracha L. Ettinger. In her book *Womanliness as Masquerade*, Riviera suggests that for competent, 'intellectual' women: "Womanliness...could be assumed and worn as a mask, both to hide the possession of masculinity and to avert the reprisals expected if she was found to possess it —much as a thief will turn out his pockets and ask to be searched to prove that he has not the stolen goods." The mask, therefore, becomes a defence mechanism against our own raw sexuality, our desires and urges, even our intelligence. It is the acceptable public face of femininity, whether in a Pre-Raphaelite painting, an airbrushed photograph of Kate Moss or in little porcelain figurines.

In 2001 Elaine Wilson travelled to Italy on a bursary from the JD Fergusson trust and visited Palermo, Florence and Rome, which deepened her interests in pattern, print, decoration and women's traditional craft skills. Influenced by the Italian Baroque she made a series of small canvases that used photographs, stitching and fabric. She also became interested in 'the sumptuous and seductive' qualities of the work of Gustav Klimt, attracted to the 'underlying tension' she found in his sensual paintings. Whilst in Sicily she photographed a marble portrait by the Renaissance sculptor Francesco Laurana in the Museum of Art in Palermo. Although very much of its time she felt it communicated "a presence and a sense of self...an art of quiet serenity and detachment." Later she found another work by him in the Victoria and Albert Museum, which led her to use her photographs of his marble portraits as the basis of a number of her collaged works, and to bring to them "a sense of connectedness between the past and present." Her work with the group The Pattern Lab led to an increased interest in the female crafts of sewing, cutting and making, which she began to explore in a series of collages. *Everything in the Garden was Rosy 2009* and *Sitting Pretty 2009* both "play with notions of artifice and deception, confinement and domesticity from a particularly female perspective." Constructed by cutting images of intricate lace patterns that echo the lace-maker's repetition and painstaking attention to detail, Wilson cuts layers of paper which are then overlapped to create different depths and points of focus, as each layer opens to reveal the underlying structures half hidden beneath. The effect of mystery, of something hidden is then heightened by coating the layers of collage with resin to make them reflective and glossy, whilst also turning the patterned layers beneath into a transparent palimpsest. Thus the image of the face "competes for attention against the pattern as if coming up for air – craving visibility." These Ophelia like visions, therefore, suggest many readings: nature versus artifice, suffocation versus freedom, even life and death.

During her time as Norma Lipman Fellow in Ceramic and Sculpture at Newcastle University, Elaine Wilson, after many years of having worked with clay and ceramics, began to revisit the subtle politics of ceramic ornamentation in the context of vanity and masquerade. As a younger artist she had been concerned, in those more rigorously feminist times, of making work that could have related to her mother or grandmother, or that might have been seen as too 'female'. With maturity she has found her own language; exploring ideas about women and femininity without resorting to either dogma or cliché. Her work is gritty, uncomfortable and probing. It asks questions about who we are and how we see ourselves within the confines of our commodified society. Subtle, complex and multilayered, it sneaks up on us to take us by surprise, lulling us with its decorative beauty, whilst pulling a punch like an iron fist in a very elegant velvet glove.

Sue Hubbard is an award-winning poet, short-story writer, novelist and freelance art-critic. Her suite of poems, written on the west coast of Ireland, 'The Idea of Islands' (Occasional Press) with drawings by the artist Donald Tesky is published in spring 2010, as are her "Adventures in Art: selected writings 1990-2010" (Other Criteria).

 Seeing Myself Seeing, 2009, fired clay, decals, perspex

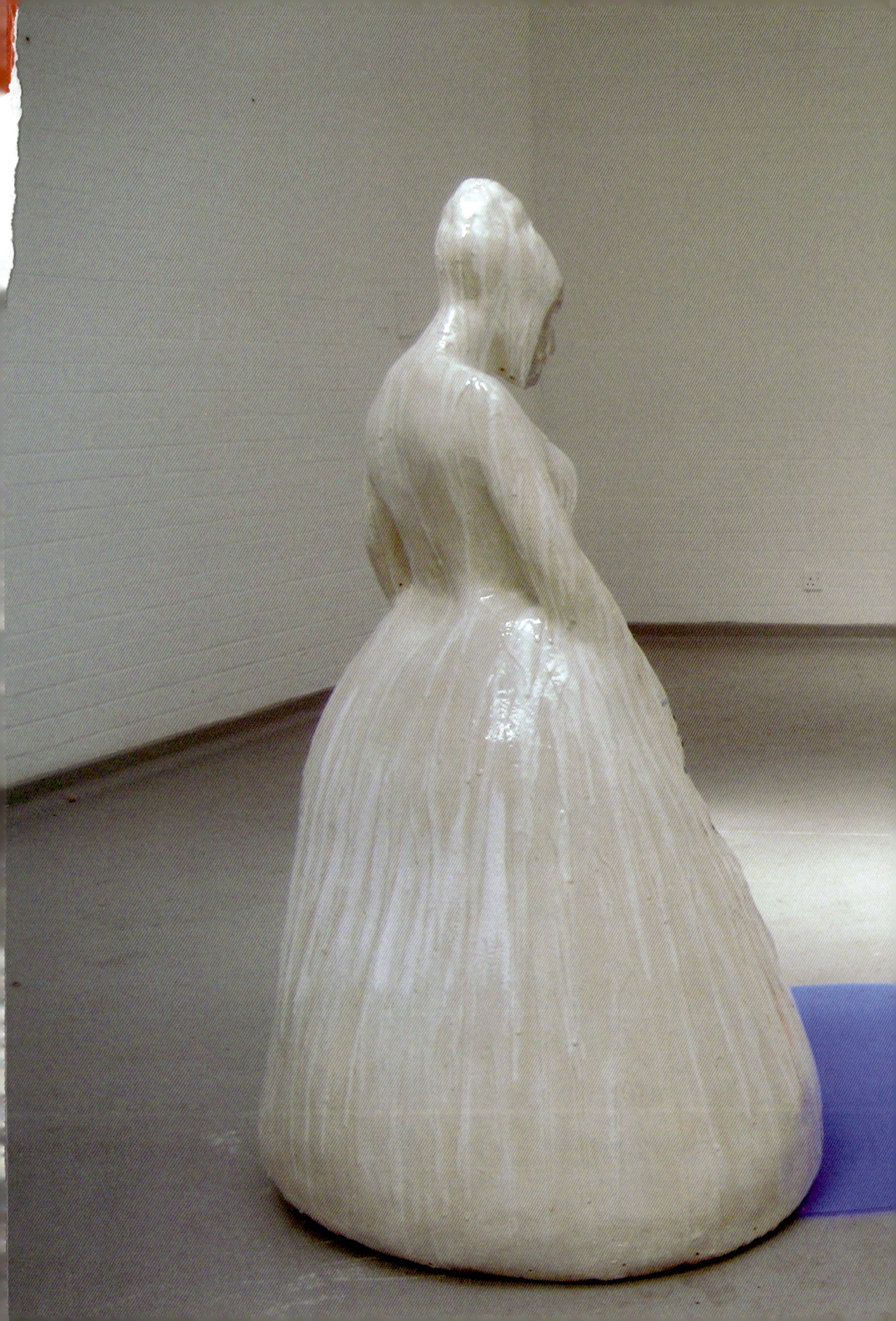

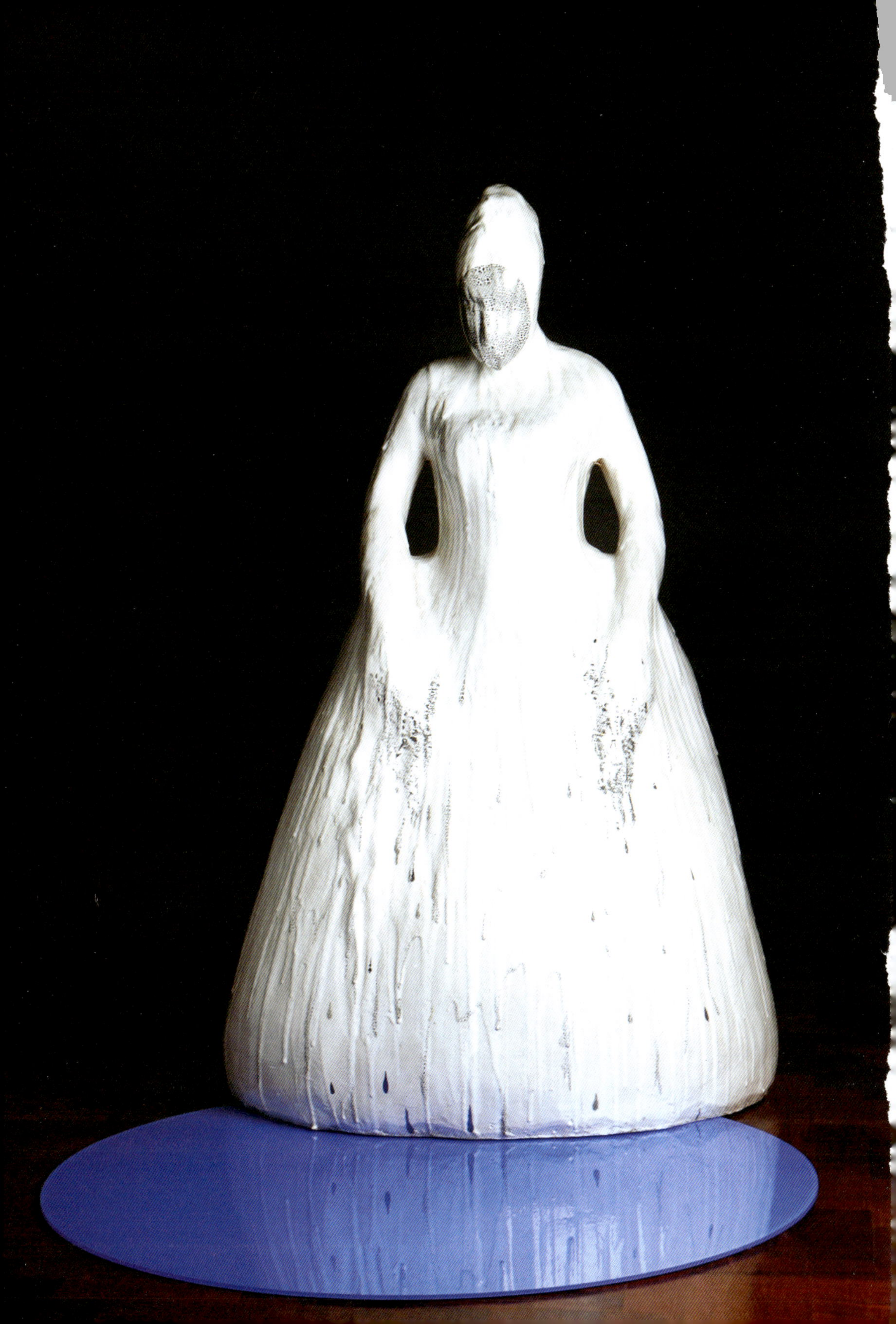

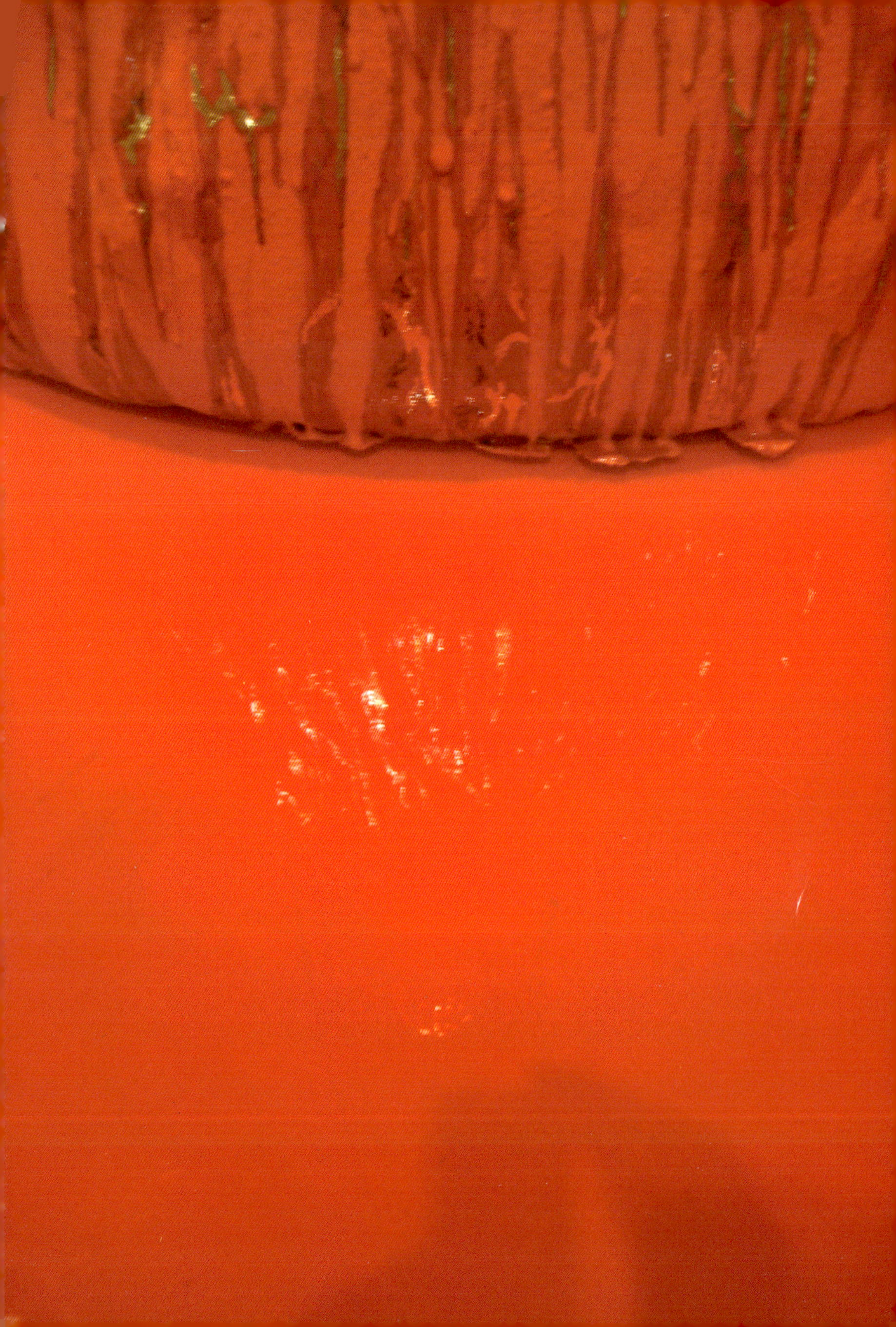

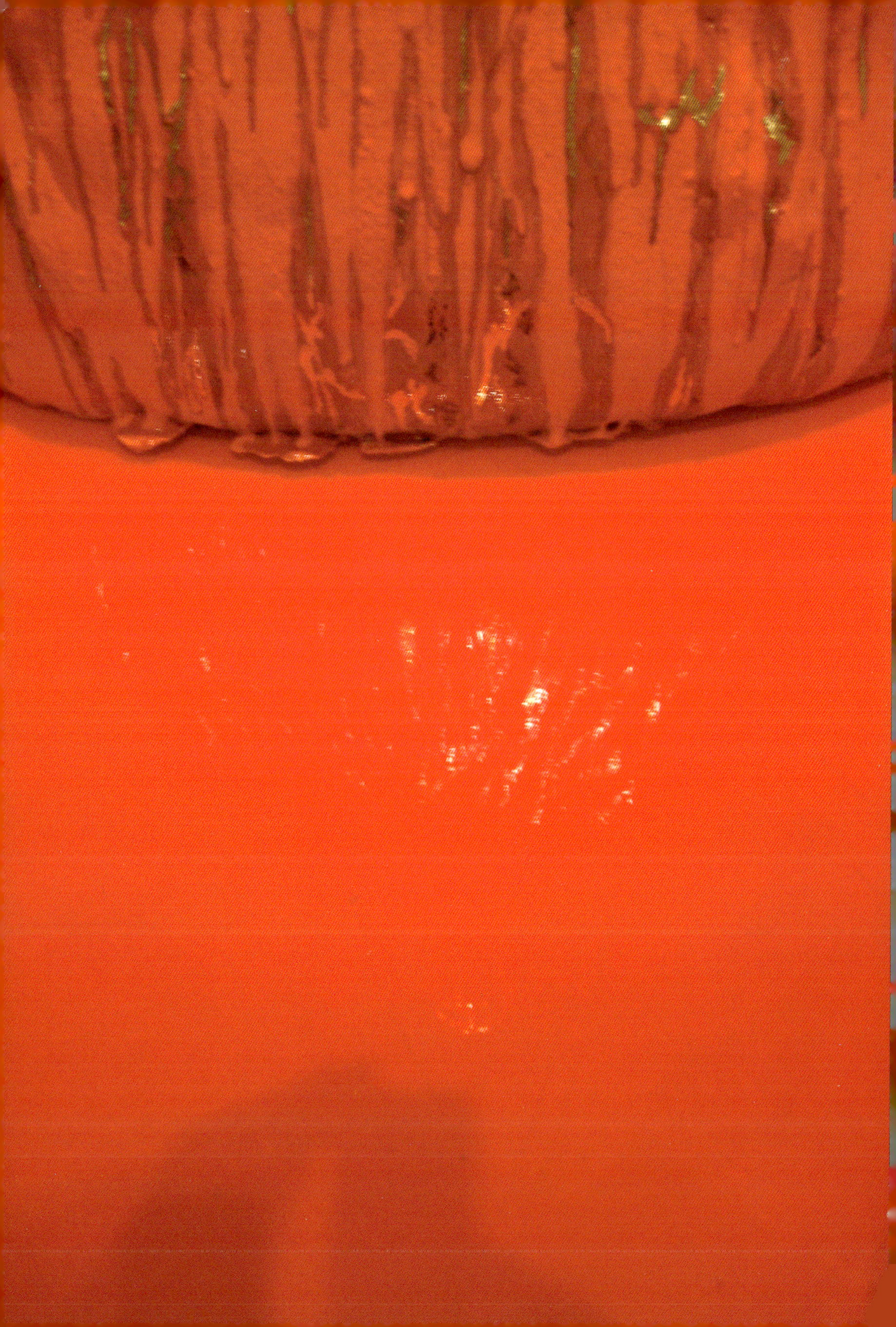

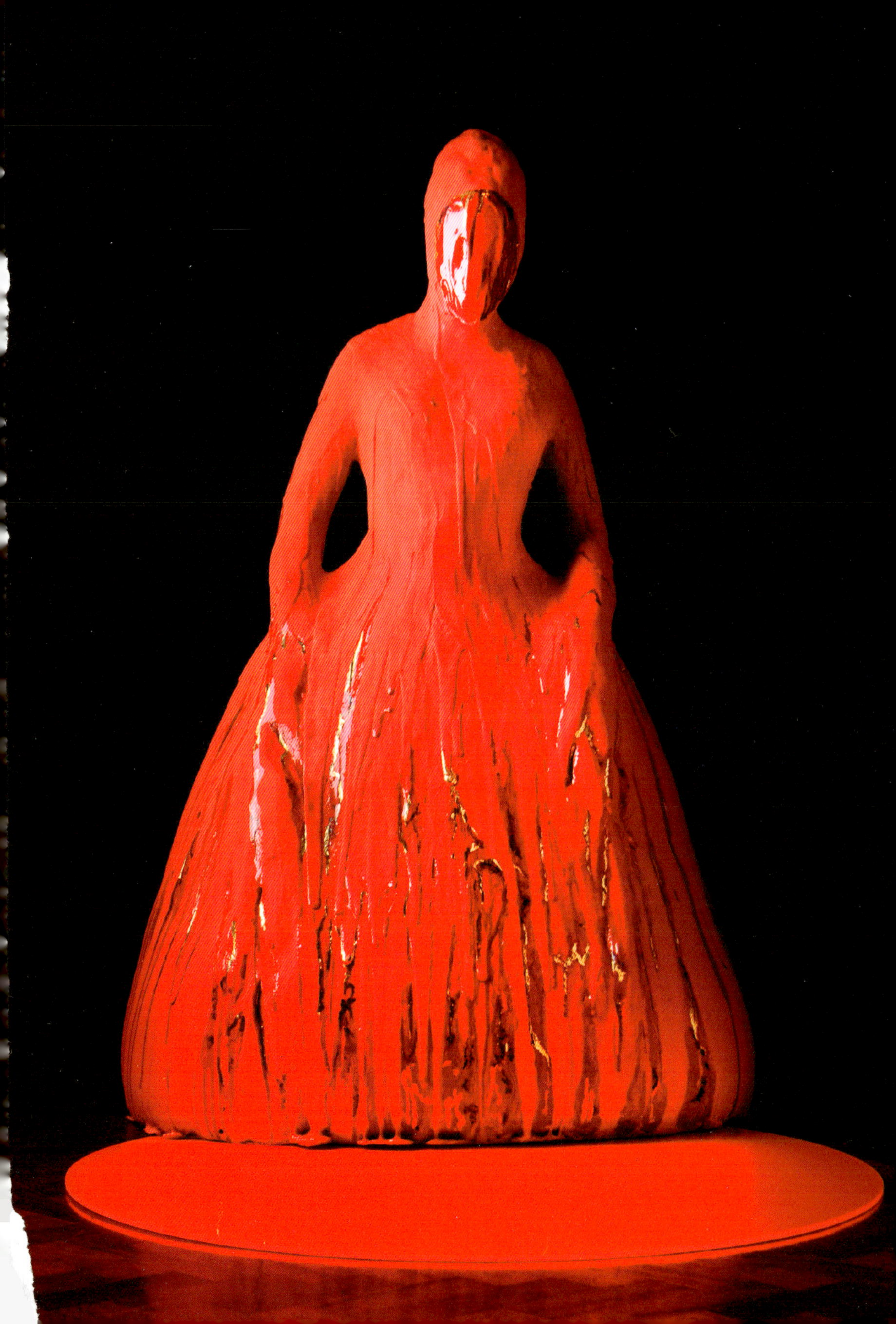

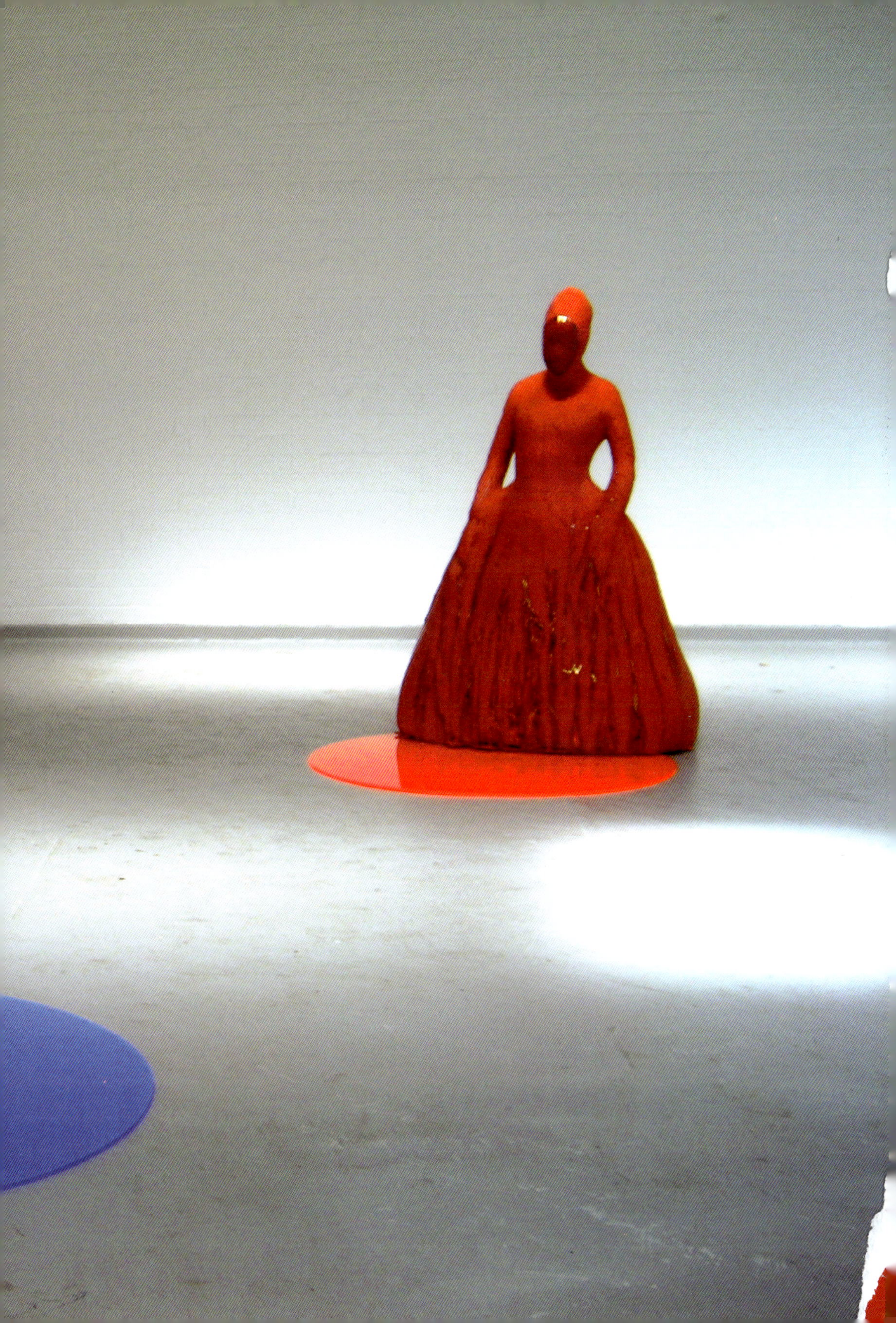

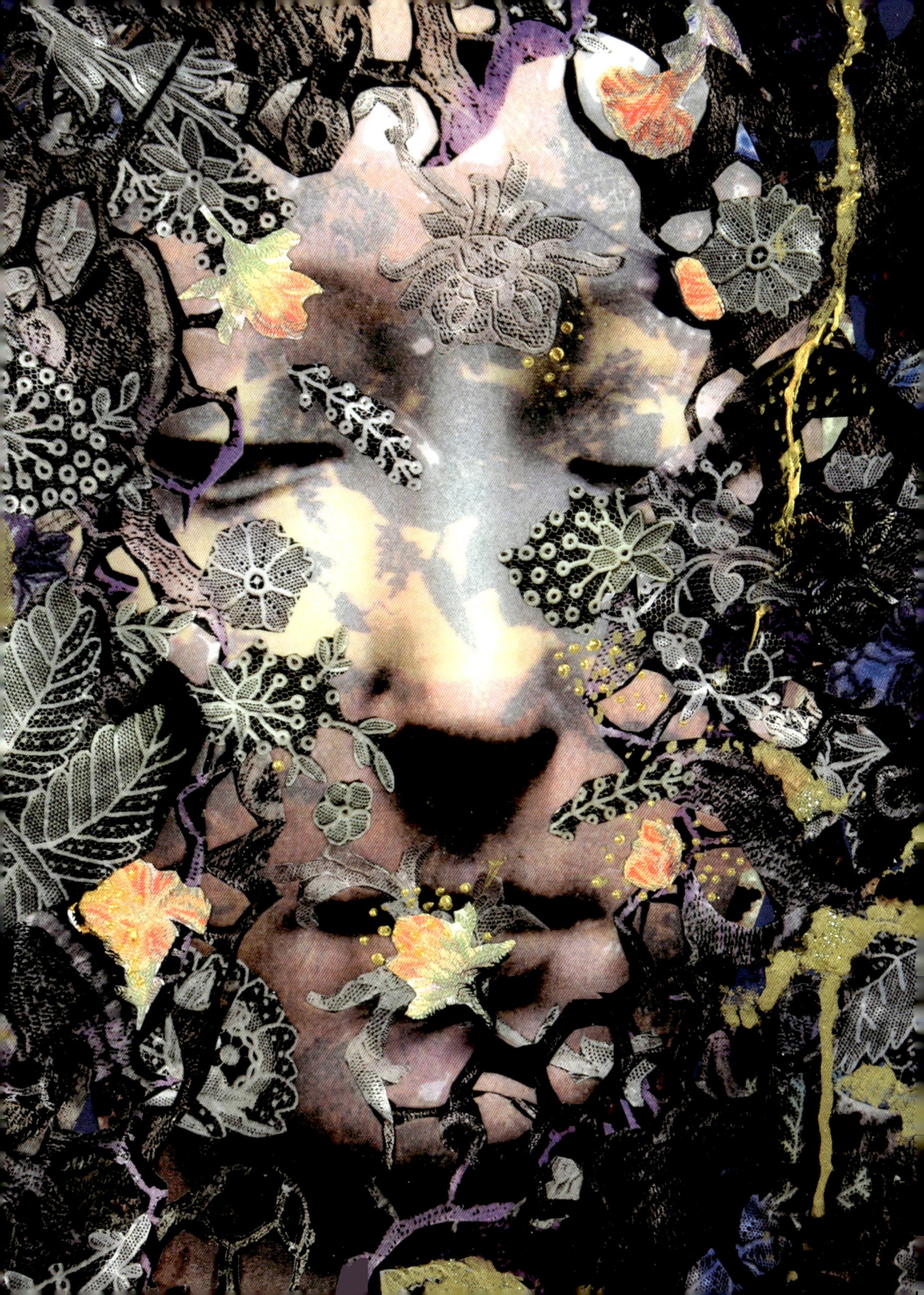

Previous: *Sipping Nectar*, 2006, (detail). Mixed media, resin

 Opposite: *Fleurs du Mal Series*, 2008-9, fired clay, glaze decals, lustre, wooden plant stands

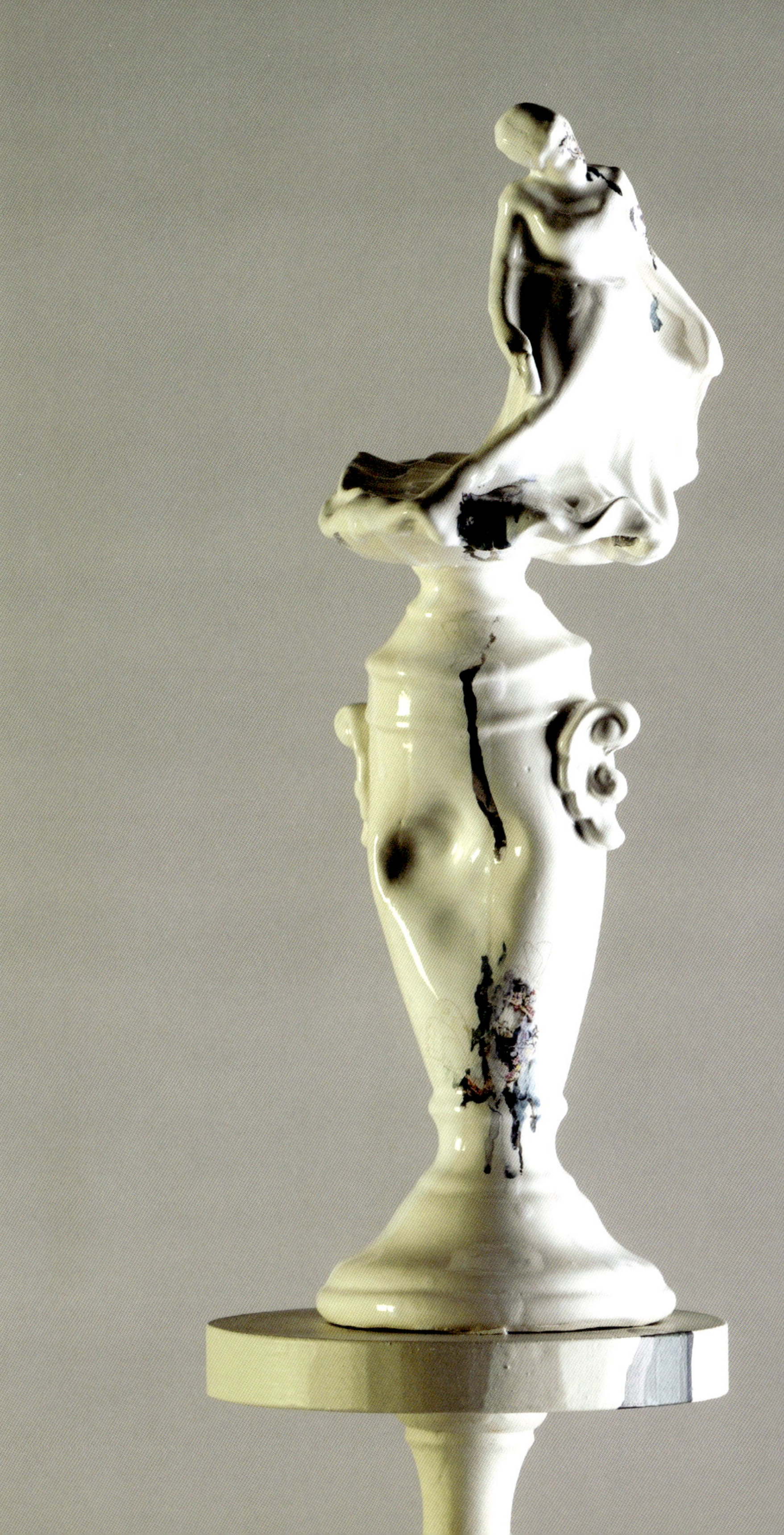

 Opposite: *Everything in the Garden was Rosy*, 2007, (detail) Mixed media, resin

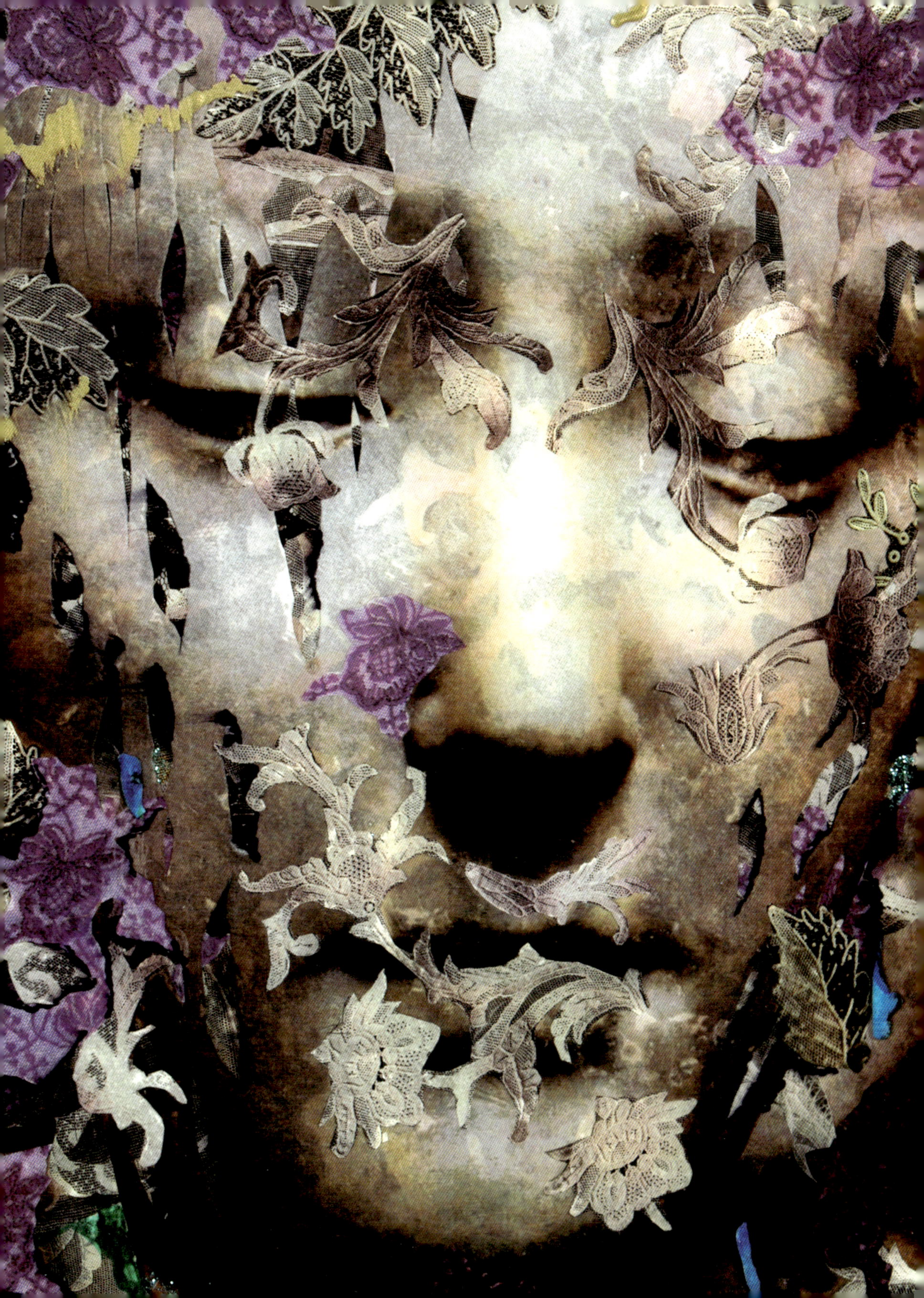

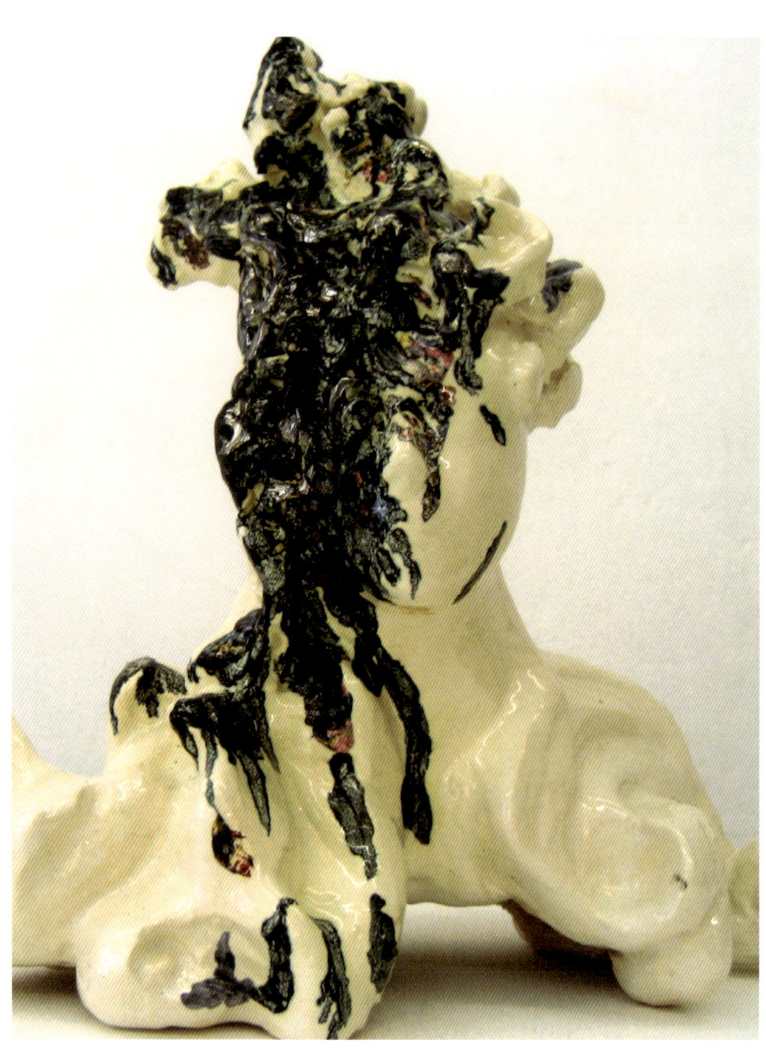

Above: *In the Blink of an Eye*, 2008, fired clay, glaze, decals, lustre
Opposite: *In Clover*, 2006, Mixed media, resin

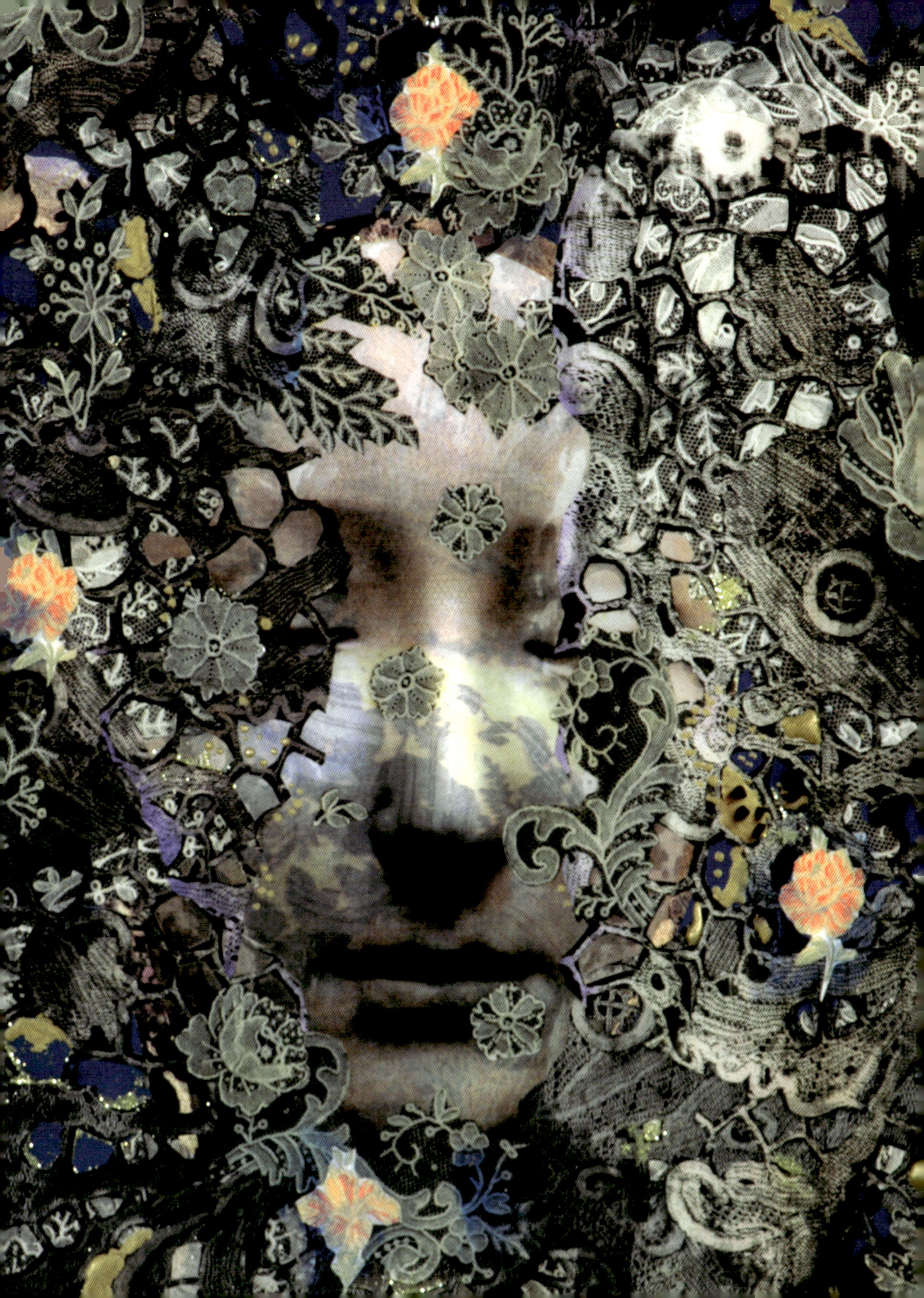

 Opposite: *I am Never the Same Person*, 2006, (detail) Mixed media, resin

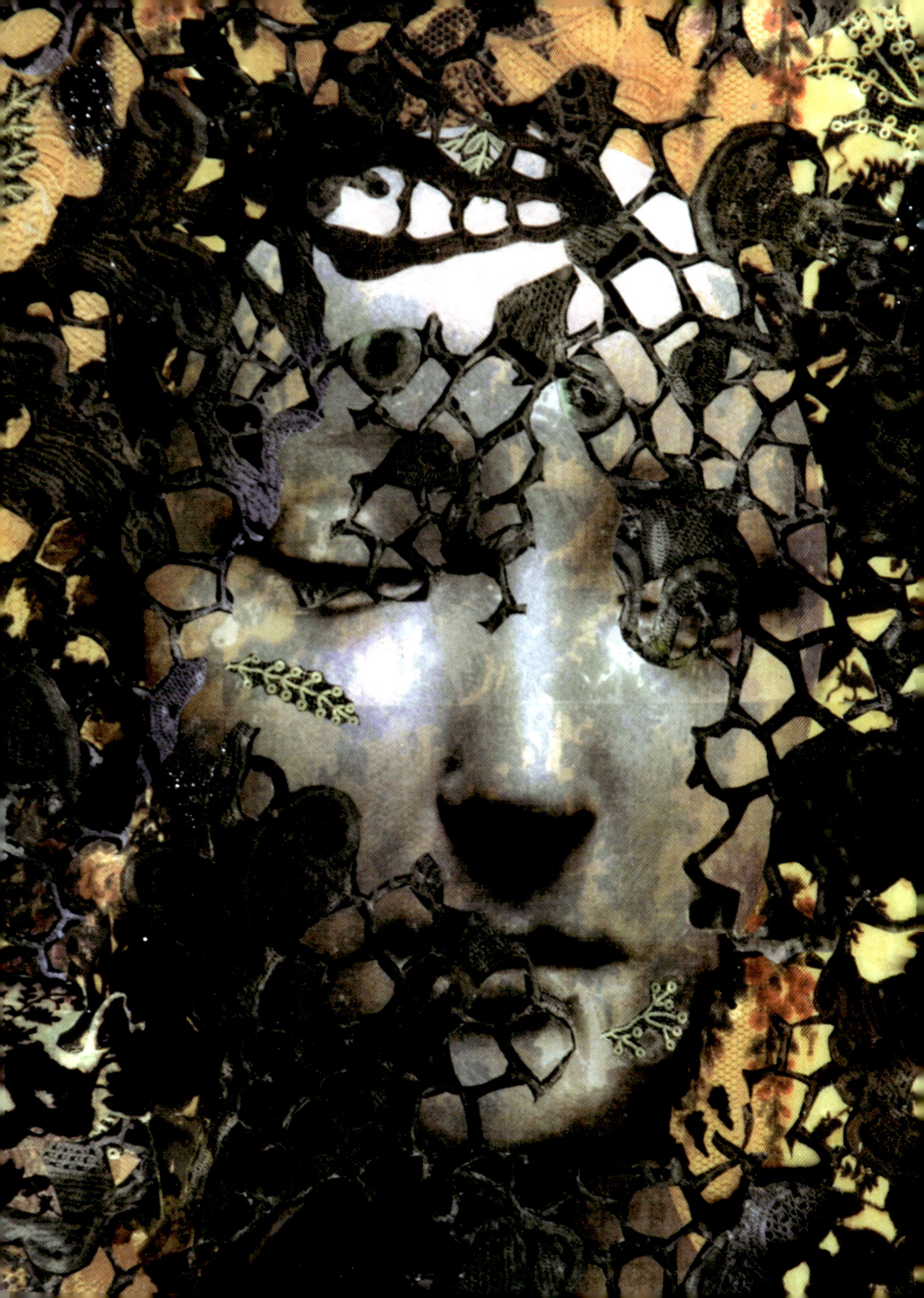

Opposite: *Now You See Me*, 2007, Mixed media, resin
Over: *A Swarm of Follies*, 2007, (detail) Mixed media, resin

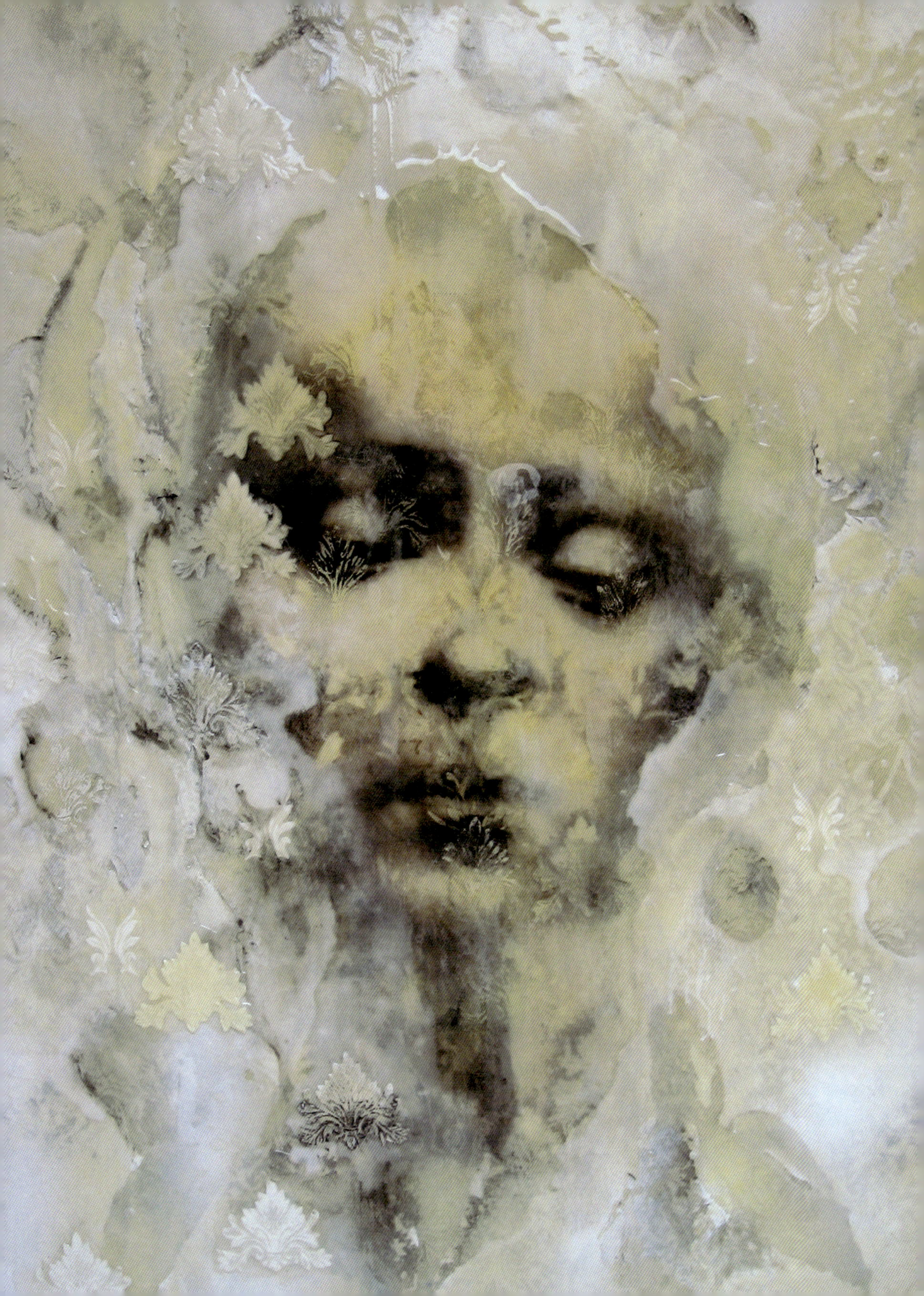

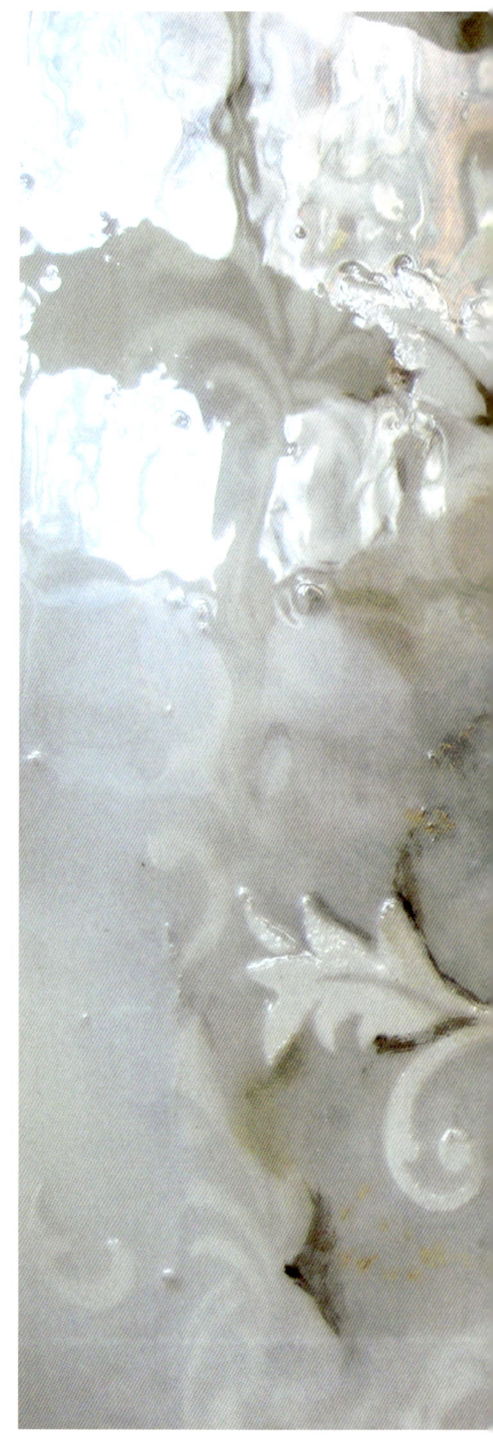

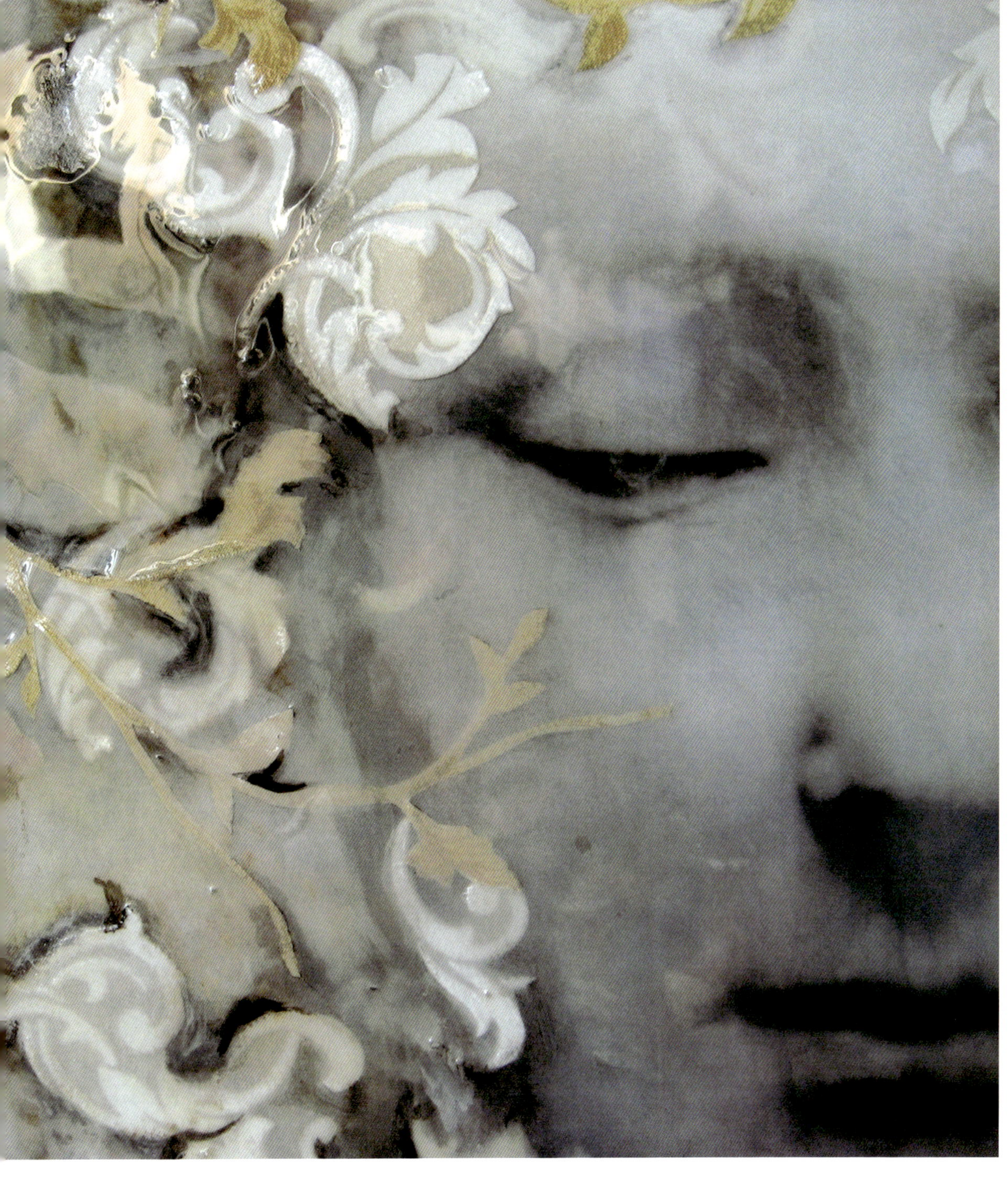

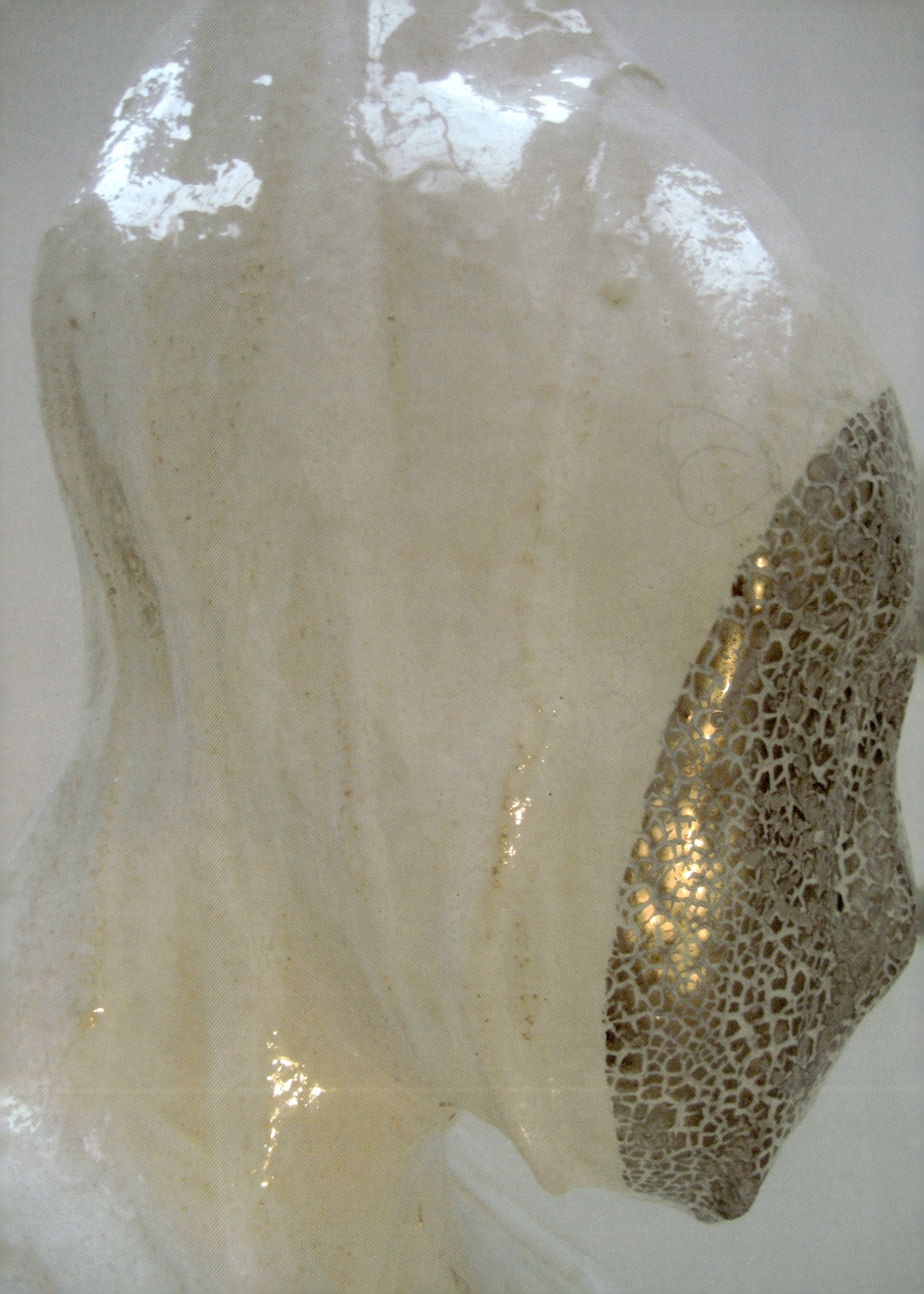

SEEING DOUBLE

> His cue, which was to perfect an imitation of myself, lay both in words and in actions: and most admirably did he play his part.[1]

In the context of attempting to write an essay about the working and aesthetic processes of another it is interesting to consider the role of stepping into another's shoes; of attempting to see through their eyes; of becoming their consciousness or at least locating yourself there or in their-abouts. By way of such a process (or processing of ideas) ¬– if successful – is an opportunity, however brief, for an artist to find themselves seeing what they are perceived to see. Whether it is a case of seeing the artist in the work, perceiving the artist behind the work or simply seeing and reading the work of the artist, for the artist – seeing yourself and your ideas redoubled and translated into words, reflected for others to read – potentiates a seldom-felt opportunity of *Seeing myself Seeing*. I hope therefore, in what unfolds below there exists some likeness, for you Elaine, in what is seen-to-be-seen.

* * * * * * * *

* * * * * * *

* * * * * * * *

As with the stated intent of this discourse – being to impart a reflection of the artist/work – it is one piece, or one installation in particular, *Seeing myself Seeing* (2009), around which I intend to develop this discussion.

Edgar Allan Poe's eponymous tale of William Wilson, details the protagonists enforced acceptance of the existence of his Double, his counterpart, his doppelganger, his other-self[2] to fatal and horrific consequence. In this portrait of likeness and difference, Poe personifies the inner voice, the conscious self of William Wilson into a quasi-physical persona – a reflected rival that is both a worthy match, and an arch nemesis. By way of his counterpart – the second William Wilson – Wilson is forced 'in a secret communion' to see himself, objectively, out with, and yet within, his own self. As the story draws to its fatal conclusion, William Wilson is in the final moments able to resolve the riddle seeing himself both for his-self and his other-self: unmasked, uncloaked and undone. It is in this final moment of existential clarity, as if in an unto then unseen mirror that Wilson, like Wilson, is able to see himself as he sees himself or is seen.

now stood where none had been perceptible before … mine own image … Thus it appeared, I say, but was not. It was my antagonist – it was Wilson, who then stood before me [3]

Whether William or Elaine, within the mise-en-scène of *Seeing myself Seeing* Wilson stands statuesque, afacing Wilson. Deadlocked at an impasse, the two figures stand firm, frozen in a Medusa's stare. Perhaps, if music were to begin, they could freely move once more, but as is they remain locked in stalemate. Stood at opposites, facing each other both the seeing and the seen are at once visible, visible to each other and visible to themselves. Castrated, vexed and negated, their blank expressionless faces bear the horror of self-recognition as they clutch on to the dying seconds of their existence. *The Double* – as described by Borges in *The Book of Imaginary Beings* – or the wraith, is 'the apparition thought to be seen by a person in his exact image just before death'. And it is *The Double*, the seeing (of the) double that seemingly manifests in *Seeing Myself Seeing* and unwittingly affects the denouement to Poe's tale; 'not a line in all the marked and singular lineaments of his face which was not, even in the most absolute identity, *mine own*!'[4]

* * * * * * * *

* * * * * * *

* * * * * * * *

Lewis Carrol's, *Through The Looking-Glass*, similarly projects and affects two sides of reality: a duality of existence in which a fictive-reality is a preposition for a contra-reality; where meaning is offset by contradiction – Tweedledum with Tweedledee and *Contrariwise* – and where all is not black and white, but red and white.

The two queens looked at each other, and the Red Queen remarked with a little shudder, 'She says she only said "if" ______'

'But she said a great deal more than that!' the White Queen moaned, wringing her hands. 'Oh, ever so much more than that!'[5]

Once more it maybe suggested that the two figures stood at the centre of *Seeing Myself Seeing* cut a sharp resemblance to characters from another place – to Carrol's Red Queen and White Queen. Both are Regal in dress; both are draped in a full-bodied couture that prudently covers every inch from the crown of each Queen's head to the base of her ankle. Shrouding the head and skirting the floor all that remains uncloaked is a countenance of a featureless visage. Within this symmetry, each Queen is a perfect counter to their opposite part; simultaneously contrasting and complimenting the other. It is not however on the black and white chequerboard squares of the chessboard that these figures sit, poised to glide into battle, but upon a perfect circle that they rest – a pool of colour that spills out from beneath the hemline and into the space in front. Part silhouette, part shadow, it is upon the opaque meniscus, upon the footprint of these giant red and blue Tiddlywinks that each Queen is vehemently and respectively rooted.

Here there can be no game plan. There is no free space onto which to make the next move; neither Red Queen nor White can move off their allotted space; no further worthwhile action is left be made, it is a stalemate. In its place unfolds a staring war, an unending blinking game, a perpetual purgatory in which both Queens have met their match. Strict rules in force: no blinking, no winking, no faces to be made; no contact at all to be had and distance to be maintained at all times. Forced to stop and stare, to see and be seen by one's own gaze, Red Queen and White Queen alike are aghast to discover, reflected across the invisible axis of symmetry, not their opposite number, their corresponding piece, but a reflection that is and can only be their other self. Fallen at their feet like Narcissus gazing at his own reflection in a forest pool, is a likeness of each, a ghostly silhouette, which unlike the statue opposite is unique to themselves – the otherness that they are not, nor will they ever become; a Double that compliments and contrasts all that they are, and all that they do. 'Gazing into the eyes that were no eyes', that is how Narcissus' 'own eyes destroyed him':

> You are Me. Now I see that.
> I see through my own reflection.
> But it is too late.[6]

[1] Edgar Allan Poe, 'William Wilson', The Masque of the Red Death, London: Penguin Books, 2008.
[2] See Jorge Luis Borges, 'The Double', The Book of Imaginary Beings, London: Vintage, 2002.
[3] Edgar Allan Poe, 'William Wilson', The Masque of the Red Death, London: Penguin Books, 2008.
[4] Edgar Allan Poe, 'William Wilson', The Masque of the Red Death, London: Penguin Books, 2008.
[5] Lewis Carrol, Through the Looking-Glass, London: Cathay Books, 1986.
[6] Ted Hughes, 'Echo and Narcissus', Tales from Ovid, London: Faber and Faber, 1997.

Matthew Hearn is a writer, curator, lecturer and sometime artist based in Newcastle upon Tyne. He has a background in fine art and is currently completing an AHRC Collaborative Doctoral Award in partnership with University of Sunderland and Locus+ Archive. He has worked with Locus+ since 2004 and currently lectures, part-time in the Fine Art Department at Newcastle University.

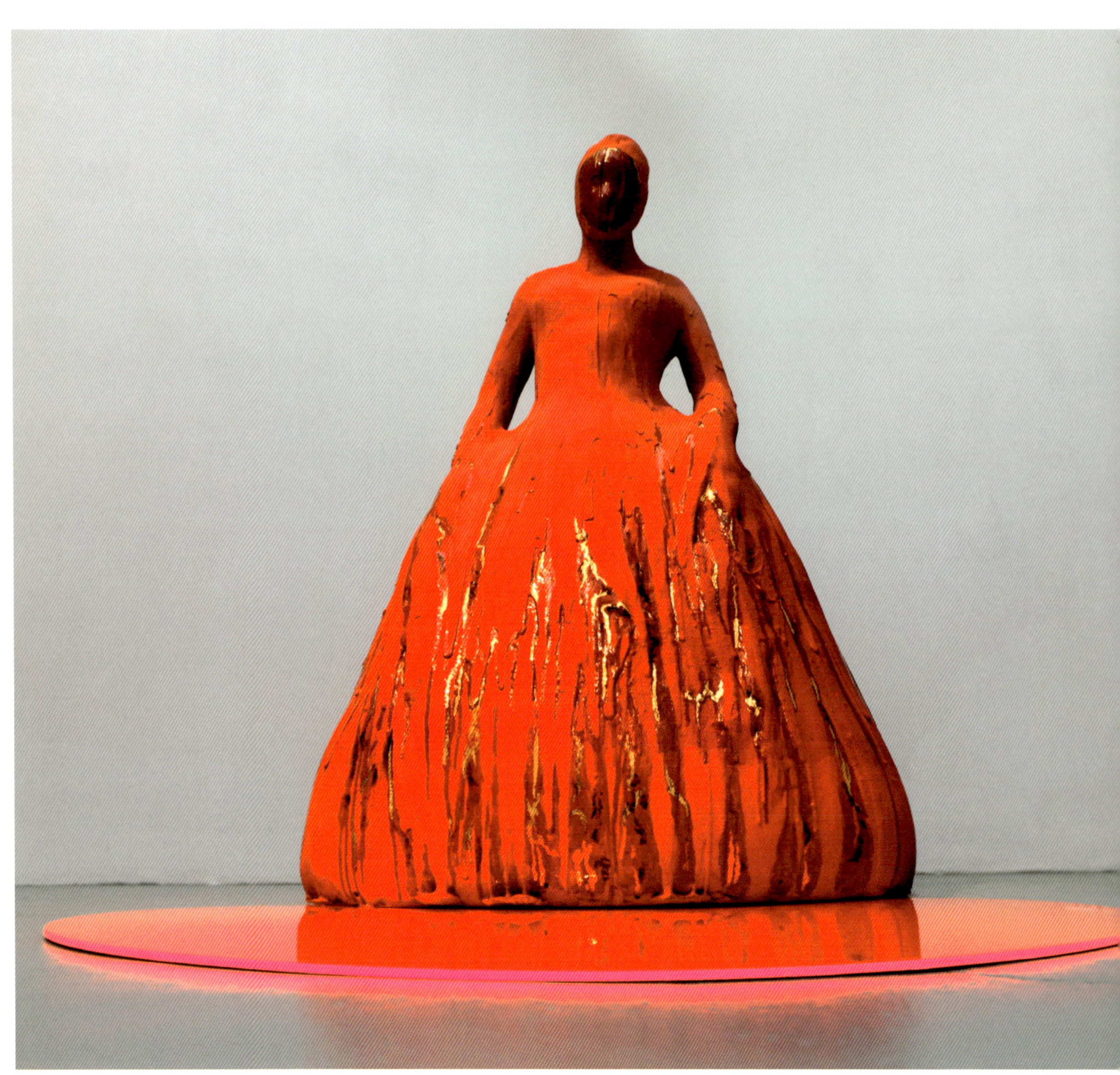

 Seeing Myself Seeing, 2009, (detail,red figure)

BIOGRAPHY

Elaine Wilson was born in Kilmarnock, Scotland. the niece of Neo-Romantic painter Robert Colquhoun. She studied sculpture at Duncan of Jordanstone School of Art in Dundee and the Royal Academy Schools in London. She has exhibited widely in Europe and America, taught in Barcelona and Florence, and has been a visiting tutor at art colleges throughout the UK. She is presently a senior lecturer in sculpture at City and Guilds of London Art School, London.

Much of Wilson's work has been made from fired clay. In 1995 she was awarded a residency at the European Ceramic Work Centre in Holland. Subsequently she was selected for an international exhibition of ceramic sculpture in Alden Biesen Castle in Belgium. This was followed on her return to Britain by two exhibitions entitled "Prime", one at the Royal Society of British Sculptors, where she exhibited a series of 50 porcelain wall objects, the other at The Poole Study Gallery. In 1996 a work was acquired for the South East Arts collection.

In 2001 a travel bursary to Italy from the JD Fergusson Trust allowed her to visit Rome, Florence and Palermo, where she embarked on a series of small stitched canvases, influenced by the Italian Baroque and the anatomical wax models of La Specola Museum. This work evolved into a significant series of intricate resin collages exploring pattern, stitch and fabric, leading to inclusion in 'Fabric' at Abbot Hall in Kendall, an exhibition that questioned the notion of decorative art as secondary to fine art. These works were further exhibited at England & Co Gallery, London.

In 2008 Wilson was awarded the Norma Lipman Research Fellowship spending a year as artist in residence in ceramic sculpture at Newcastle University. During this year she explored variations on the figurine, the romantic ideal and ideas on femininity drawn from the writing of Bracha-Ettinger, Joan Riviere and Baudelaire. While inevitably addressing feminist issues, she was primarily interested in the philosophical debates of self-reflection and 'otherness', ideas reflected in the large sculpture 'Seeing Myself Seeing'.

The residency in Newcastle concluded in an exhibition at the Hatton Gallery, entitled 'Spoiled', an exhibition of collages 'A Swarm of Follies' at The Globe Gallery and further exhibitions at the GiftGallery10 Vyner Street, London, and at Bath Spa University Gallery in May 2010.

The exhibitions and catalogue have been supported by the Arts Council, The Hope ScottTrust, the Lipman Trust, Newcastle University and Kingston University.

Art Editions North
Peter Davies

First published in 2008 by Art Editions North c/o Faculty of Arts, Design & Media, University of Sunderland, Ashburne House, Ryhope Road, Sunderland SR2 7EF.
tel: +44 (0) 191 515 2128

Photography Elaine Wilson apart from Colin Davison (pgs 3, 4, 7, 10, 13, 15, 16, 31, insideflaps gatefold) & Niall Buchanan (pgs 29, 35, 37) & Gift 10 Vyner St (pg 46)

British Library Cataloguing-in-Publication Data
A British Library CIP record is available

ISBN 978 0 9557478 4 7

Design: Joanna Deans, joannadeans@mac.com
Printing: Stewarts of Edinburgh

Distributed by Cornerhouse Publications
70 Oxford Street, Manchester M1 5NH, England
tel: +44 (0) 161 200 1503, fax: +44 (0) 161 200 1504
email: publications@cornerhouse.org
www.cornerhouse.org/publishers

The artist would like to thank, The Hatton Gallery, The Norma Lipman Bequest, Gift 10 Vyner St, Matthew Hearn, Jo Deans, Peter Davies, Kingston University, Photography Dept, Susan, Bruce and Ollie. Also for their unwavering support and help over the years Lorna Gibson, Alistair and Diane Wilson, Jenny Tylden-Wright.

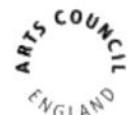

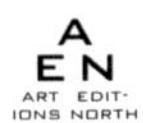

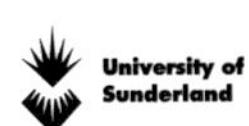

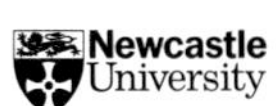

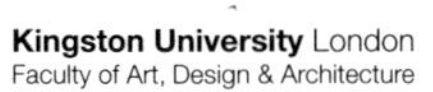

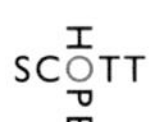